SINGLES
Ministry Resources

Building COMMUNITY

Joel Walker
&
Kent McIlhaney

David C. Cook

Building Community
© 1998 David C. Cook Church Ministries,
a division of Cook Communications

Cable address: DCCOOK
Series creator: Jerry Jones
Series editor: Gary Wilde
Designer: Joanna Shafer
Cover illustrator: Don Pierce

Unless otherwise noted, Scripture quotations are from the Holy Bible, New International Version
(NIV), ©1973, 1978, 1984 by International Bible Society.
Used by permission of Zondervan Bible Publishers.

Published by Cook Communications Ministries
4050 Lee Vance View
Colorado Springs, CO 80918

Printed in U.S.A.

ISBN: 0-7814-5426-3

CONTENTS

About the Authors

Kent McIlhaney works as the High Adventure Director for Peak 3 Outfitters, a ministry in Colorado Springs, Colorado. He holds college degrees in theology (Bethel College, Minnesota) and Physical Education (Northeastern Illinois University) and has begun graduate work in Adventure Education at Chicago State University. Kent has 15 years of experience working in Christian camping. He enjoys playing hockey, skiing, and just being outdoors.

Joel Walker is the CEO of Peak 3 Outfitters and is committed to building teams for Jesus Christ. The team that Joel enjoys working with the most is his family—his wife Shelly and his four daughters. Joel is a golf fanatic and knows there are golf courses in Heaven (though he's hoping for a delayed "tee time").

WELCOME TO...
An exciting study experience with your singles!

Wethink you've made an excellent choice with Single Adult Ministry Studies leader's guides. In this series, you have a single focus with multiple options format, designed to build healthy relationships and deal with relevant topics for today's single adults—all from a biblical perspective.

The concept for this series is the result of in-depth explorations with singles ministry leaders from across the country. In focus groups and one-on-one interviews, these experts "on the front lines" of single adult Christian education told us what they need and want for their groups. As a result, you get the most practical activities and the most relevant, up-to-date discussions of constantly requested topics.

The volumes in this series are for singles groups from every age group, background, denomination, and life situation. We've targeted, in particular, single adults ages 25-32 (although we fully expect that this series will be enjoyed by older singles, as well). No matter who is in your group, make everyone feel welcomed and appreciated. And use your session plans as the springboard for genuine, open communication and discussion.

Using This Guide

You'll soon realize that SAM Studies are extremely flexible and adaptable to your particular needs. That's because the three Instruction Pages in each session let you plan for a variety of time frames and settings:

- A "Short Course,"— as in a Sunday school Bible study (35-45 minutes); or
- A Small Group Setting—either in a home or as a "break out" from a larger group (60-90 minutes); or
- A Large Group Setting—for an Extended Weeknight Program or Retreat Setting (two hours or more).

Single ministry leaders have indicated again and again that they want the material to be easy to use in any one of these three settings. After all, volunteers are often leading the group—people who may not take the time to read the entire course. These leaders often just want the material for the meeting they are responsible for. As a result, this series is designed to make preparation as complete and organized as possible. It all begins with becoming familiar with how each session is put together...

Session Intro / Overview Page. This is your introduction to the study topic, giving you an interest-grabbing overview, Session Aim, Key Concepts, and Bible References.

Instruction Pages. Here you'll find three different sets of instructions, depending on the size, setting, and time requirements of your particular group. Choose the session that's best for you!

My Personal Game Plan. This is your personal session-planning page. It helps you organize the activities and options you've chosen, step by step. It also includes "Just for You"—a short devotional exercise to prepare your own heart for leading the session.

Looking to the Word. This step lays out the key themes that should flow from your time together. It's actually a mini-lecture that is "presentation based"—given to you exactly as you might present it to your group. Of course, you'll want to make it your own by studying it thoroughly and adding personal anecdotes and illustrations to make it sing!

This section includes Going Deeper. It provides informative "nuggets" related to the textual, cultural, or historical background of the Bible passages. The singles ministry leaders we interviewed said: "Give me information that helps me look like an expert."

Extra Options Pages. These two pages list several additional options for use with steps 1, 3, 4 and 5. Go here when you're looking for a broader range of active alternatives for group participation.

Reproducible Interactive Pages. These are your reproducible handouts, to be used by group members during the session. Interactive Page #1 goes with the short meeting time setting. Interactive Page #2 goes with the small group setting. You'll find group activities, individual exercises, and discussion questions here.

Take Home Page (front and back). Use this page as a kind of bulletin insert that group members can take home with them. It will help "set the hook" on the Key Concepts you've conveyed during your session. Occasionally, it will also offer activities to be used in the session itself.

So . . . once you know how everything's organized, you'll lead your group through five steps in each session. These steps are clearly laid out on the Instruction Page you choose for your group and setting.

Take Note!

Pay special attention to these items in your SAM leader's guide, and become familiar with how to use them in the most effective ways.

- About the Options. Feel free to insert them wherever you think they'd work the best for you. The idea is for you to build a lesson plan from the "menu of methods" we've provided. Go for it!

- About the Icons. Notice that the icons on the Instruction Pages visually coordinate with the Interactive Pages you'll use them with. Just another way to help you stay organized.

- About the Take Home Pages. You'll photocopy these pages for everyone— back-to-back, if possible, to make a single handout sheet. That way, group members can fold them and use them as an insert in their Bibles during the week ahead.

• About "Presenting What the Bible Has to Say." We want you to be an expert presenter during the Bible content portion of your session. That's why we give you the outlines and illustrations you can use to make everything flow in a smooth and interesting mini-talk. Just go over the material thoroughly and adjust it here and there to truly make it your own.

Building Community in Your Singles Group

How do you build a sense of community in your group? It's a challenge every singles ministry leader faces. The fact is, singles are living the single life. Many approach their problems in an individualistic way—out of necessity. Yes, many have come to see that a few solid, caring relationships are essential to their survival. Still others have built incredibly strong ties of friendship or enjoy loving relationships among many relatives. But nevertheless, the focus often comes down to: "Me against the world."

Yet the biblical vision of the body of Christ is the functioning together of all the members to do the will of God in His kingdom. And that is the focus of this volume of studies on building community. It's learning to view one another as members together in the body. Learning to think of the group working as a unit to accomplish God's will. Learning to trust that as we share deeply of our lives together, we will grow to depend on one another for emotional and spiritual support. In this way, your singles will come to know that they can seek God's will, not only through a person relationship with Him, but by going to one another for the discernment and wisdom that God has given their brothers and sisters in Christ. After all, this is so often how God speaks to us and leads us— through the encouraging wisdom of a fellow believer.

Building community requires increasing doses of mutual trust. That's why these sessions are filled with trust games and group challenges that demand teamwork. This is an active study series. It gets your group members moving around, touching one another, pulling together. It's not just a cognitive exercise; it requires committing to and knowing one another at increasingly deeper levels. The exercises and activities should help you do that, but feel free to adapt them and make them fit your group's particular personality. And whatever you do, keep pushing the idea that we are all in this together.

Other Books in the SAM Studies series—

Living in an Uncertain World (Studies in the Book of Ruth)
Discovering God's Design on Your Life
Living Your Faith Inside and Out

To order by phone 1-888-888-4SAM

Session 1
A MOST EXCELLENT
Love

Love makes the world go round!

It's true, isn't it? Love is the deepest need of every human being. It's the one thing we're all seeking, with all of our hearts, in just about everything we do and say. Yet we live in an unloving world today. Many of us are actually "love starved" because of past relationships that failed to grow and deepen into the intimacy we'd hoped for. And we've often been hurt by our attempts at loving someone else.

As a result, many of us have a warped perspective on healthy brother and sister love relationships in the church. We need a better understanding of the important and powerful role love plays in awesome community.

At the conclusion of 1 Corinthians 12, the apostle Paul proclaims the most excellent way of living our lives—and his message is all about love. While Paul doesn't call love a gift, he implies it all the way through chapter 13. Therefore, though your singles bring many gifts to the table of life, they need to begin seeing love as a gift, too. It is a most awesome gift *to be given away in community.*

Yes, love makes the world go round. And it makes the church a heaven on earth. What a most excellent thing is love!

SESSION AIM

To help single adults understand that healthy love is the most excellent gift we can offer each other in community.

WHAT'S IT ALL ABOUT?

As you move through your session, keep in mind these Key Concepts you'll be conveying to your group members:

•Love is the most awesome and excellent gift we can give one another.
•Love is the fuel that makes healthy relation-ships burn bright.
•Love is the way to influence our world for Christ.

BIBLE REFERENCES:

1 Corinthians 12:31
1 Peter 3:8
John 13:35

1—Let's Get Started
(5-10 minutes)

Option 1: Your Most Awesome Gift
Needed: Half sheets of paper; a small bowl or box.

Distribute half-sheets of paper and invite each person to jot the three most awesome gifts they've received in their life time. When all have finished, place the crumbled half sheets into a bowl. Mix up the contents, and have each person pick out one paper ball (not their own). In a gathered circle, have each person read aloud the jotted gifts, with everyone trying to guess who wrote them. Finally, have persons explain *why* one or two of those gifts were so awesome.

Option 2: Gift-Wrapped Love
Needed: Boxes, wrapping paper, tags.

Wrap different-sized boxes in gift wrap, and write a tag on each one that says "To a Special Someone." Place a slip of paper in each box that says, "Say or express love to a special someone in this room." Have each person open up his or her box, read the statement, and respond.

Option 3: Discussion Questions
Use the questions on Interactive Page #1, under "Whaddaya Think." Have participants form into pairs or small groups to discuss before reporting their insights to the larger group.

Note: If time or interest allows, use additional options found on pages 17-18.

2—Looking to the Word
(15 minutes)

Present the material found in "Presenting What the Bible Has to Say," on pages 14-16. Become very familiar with these three segments, so you can offer your comments with minimal notes: (1) Introduction, (2) Key Concepts, and (3) Conclusion. Keep your presentation simple, using your own personal anecdotes to spark interest. Draw upon the "Going Deeper" information as desired.

3—Applying It to My Life
(5-10 minutes)

Needed: Paper and pencils for small groups.

As soon as you complete your presentation, split the group up into teams of four. Tell everyone that another way to look at 1 Corinthians 12 and 13 is to view Paul as a biblical "crooner"—a singer of "*agape* love songs" to the church at Corinth. Have each team brainstorm to jot a list of love songs (and remembered lyrics) from their generation. Then have them pick out the words or phrases from each love song that Paul could have used to describe love in his preaching at Corinth. Have the teams share their responses.

4—Taking the Next Step
(5 minutes)
1. Read aloud 1 Corinthians 13:4-8 from *The Living Bible* or *The Message*.
2. Use the "Love Divided" exercise on Interactive Page #1 to invite specific, practical applications.

5—Let's Wrap It Up
(5 minutes)
1. Invite your group members to see themselves as givers of the most awesome gift anyone can offer. As they pray, have them say (aloud, if possible) the names of people that they would like to give this gift to in the week ahead.
2. Pray that your surrounding community will be influenced by the love evident within your singles group. Then stand and hold hands in a circle, asking everyone to thank God for the person on his or her right.
3. Distribute the Take Home Page.

HINT:

As an option, wrap a gift for you—the leader—to open. Write on the tag, "To a special group." Think of how you would express your love for these folks—then do it.

When You Have More Time...
(How to Use This Material in 60-90 Minutes)
Example: Small Groups at Home

1—Let's Get Started
(5-10 minutes)

Option 1: Love Song Sing-Off

Split the entire group in half. Give the two teams about ten minutes to come up with as many love song titles as they can. After ten minutes, tell both groups that when you point to them, they should begin singing the first love song on their list. After they have sung a line or two of the song, tell them to stop, and then point to the other group. Continue to alternate, back and forth, moving down each group's list of songs. Compete to see which group can sing more love songs than the other, without repeating a song.

Option 2: String It Along

Needed: Several long pieces of string; same number of metal washers.

Form two or more groups. Give each group a 25-foot piece of string with a washer tied into it. Compete to see which group can move the washer around the circle the most quickly and efficiently. Time each group as they work for their best time. Then discuss:

• *What part does "cooperation and working together" play in a developing love among believers? Can you give a practical example?*

Option 3: Agree/Disagree?

Use the opinion exercise on Interactive Page #2, under "Agree or Disagree?" Tell your singles that you are going to read a series of "controversial" statements. After reading each one, ask for a show of hands indicating whether people agree or disagree with the statement. Use the statement as the basis for a discussion on the nature of genuine love.

2—Looking to the Word
(10-15 minutes)

Present the material found in "Presenting What the Bible Has to Say," on pages 14-16. Divide your allotted time into three segments: (1) Introduction, (2) Key Concepts, and (3) Conclusion.

3—Applying It to My Life
(20-25 minutes)

1. As soon as you complete your presentation, give everyone in the group a piece of paper and a pen or pencil. Have individuals address a letter to themselves (i.e., "Dear *My Name*"). When you say go, have everyone take their letter and hand it to the person to his or her left. That person then begins to write a letter to the addressed person. At your signal, each person stops writing and hands the letter to the left again. Move the letter all the way around the circle and back to the original addressee. Have people read their letters (or portions of them) aloud to the group.

2. If you will have time, refer group members to the poem "Letting Go" on Interactive Page #2. Ask your singles how they could apply the poem to their lives.

4—Taking the Next Step
(15-20 minutes)

In groups of at least three people, have each person write on a piece of paper the first name of a person in their life who needs love shown to them—and why. Put all of the papers in a cup and then pass it around, having each person remove a paper other than their own. Have each person prepare a "suggested next step" idea for the chosen group member. Take turns offering one another your practical ideas for a love-response in each situation.

5—Let's Wrap It Up
(10-20 minutes)

1. Form a circle. Then have everyone bow their heads and offer a sentence prayer beginning with one of these phrases:

I praise You for Your...
I love You for Your...
Thank You for...

2. After the sentence prayers, make your group announcements, then distribute the Take Home Page.

HINT:

Since your class is meeting for the first time, you may wish to start with an "ice-breaker" to help everyone get acquainted. Have group members sit in a circle and give each person forty-four seconds (time it!) to respond to these two statements: 1)one of the most intriguing things about me is...; 2)one reason a study on "community building" appeals to me is...

1—Let's Get Started
(20-30 minutes)

Option 1: Submarine Escape

Use one large group, or split the group into teams of six to ten people. Explain that groups must save each member of their team from a submarine compartment that is filling with water. The doors must be opened and closed quickly to prevent water from overtaking the rest of the vessel.

The team will split in half, forming two lines facing each other with their arms outstretched toward the other line. Each person's arms are between the arms of the person directly across from them. One member stands at the end of the line and prepares to walk between the line with eyes closed. When the walkers begin to walk, the people immediately in front of them raise their arms, allowing them to pass untouched. As soon as the walker passes by, the arms must be immediately lowered to prevent water from escaping. The person walking chooses how fast to walk. For safety reasons, this person should never be touched! Communicate to the group when the person is to start and stop so group members may be prepared.

After practicing this submarine escape to perfection, the group(s) can discuss:

• *How is trusting someone we love like, and unlike, trusting them with our life itself? When have you found this to be true?*

Option 2: Plug It Up
Needed: A #10 coffee can, hammer, and nail.

Divide into small groups that will compete against one another. Puncture holes in the outside of the can, about three or four holes every inch around the sides. Then suspend the can in the air or put it on a table. (You may want to do this activity outside because of the water that will be spilled.)

The groups now take turns trying to plug all the holes with their fingers in order to keep the can full for one minute without adding any water. Water may be poured

gradually into the can—or just go crazy with it and make a huge mess. After the competition, draw out the spiritual parallels by asking:

• *What things prevent our love from flowing out to others?*
• *Are we allowing God to pour His love into us? Explain.*

Note: If time or interest allows, use additional options found on pages 17-18.

2—Looking to the Word
(35 minutes)

1. You may wish to use the brief exercise titled "Finish the Thought" (on the Take Home Page) to introduce your Bible presentation.

2. Offer a brief mini-lecture using the material found in "Presenting What the Bible Has to Say," on pages 14-16.

3—Applying It to My Life
(30 minutes)

After you've offered your biblical presentation, use the optional activity titled "Measuring Up" on page 18.

4—Taking the Next Step
(40 minutes)

1. Distribute the Take Home Page and have your singles read the verses for the session again.

2. Then give everyone about ten minutes of silence to do the "Ranking Love" section on the page. Allow enough time for the discussion questions.

5—Let's Wrap It Up
(5 minutes)

1. Make announcements about coming events or activities.

2. Close by taking prayer requests in small groups and then assigning individuals to pray for each request.

My Personal Game Plan

STEP 1 — Time: _____ minutes.

Materials Needed:

Activities Summary:

STEP 2 — Time: _____ minutes.

Materials Needed:

Activities Summary:

STEP 3 — Time: _____ minutes.

Materials Needed:

Activities Summary:

STEP 4 — Time: _____ minutes.

Materials Needed:

Activities Summary:

STEP 5 — Time: _____ minutes.

Materials Needed:

Activities Summary:

Just for You
Teacher's Devotional

Someone once said, "The really important things in life can't be photographed." Love is one of those things. Its invisible power reaches deep into the core of who we are.

As part of your preparation for leading this session, prayerfully review the qualities of genuine love in 1 Corinthians 13:4-8. Then think about one person in your past who has significantly influenced you with his or her life and love. Pick out the words from verses 4 through 8 that made this person's love so powerful. For instance, was she extraordinarily patient with you? Was he a truth seeker? Consistently unselfish? Amazingly persevering?

Now ask yourself: *How would I like my love to come across to the singles I'm trying to influence for Christ in this group?* Choose three words out of the passage that describe the kind of love you want to display to your singles. Jot how those words could be displayed in practical deeds—your "wisdom-requests" here:

Word:

Deeds:

Word:

Deeds:

Word:

Deeds:

Meditate for a moment on these "words" that you want your singles to take home when they consider your love for them. And remember—many of these folks won't remember most of the things you tell them. But you can be sure they'll remember your practical, tangible expressions of caring.

—Joel and Kent

MY GOALS FOR THIS SESSION:

- TO HELP SINGLE ADULTS
  _____
  _____
  _____

- TO HELP SINGLE ADULTS
  _____
  _____
  _____

- TO HELP SINGLE ADULTS
  _____
  _____
  _____

- TO HELP SINGLE ADULTS
  _____
  _____
  _____

WHAT I LEARNED FROM READING 'LOOKING TO THE WORD'...

Notes and Insights—

LOOKING TO THE WORD—A MOST EXCELLENT LOVE

Presenting
What the Bible Has to Say...

Here's your mini-lecture covering the biblical Key Concepts. Try to become familiar with the flow of thoughts, and the outline, in order to present this material with maximum eye contact. Special instructions to you are in bold type.
(Note: Have group members refer to the Key Concepts section on their Interactive Page. They may wish to fill in the blanks as you speak.)

Introduction

Show a video clip from the movie *Hoosiers*. The section of the video to play comes at the end of the movie, right before the team's last game. Here the coach, Norman Dale, gets the team members in their final huddle, and says, "I love you guys."
You can say:

How many of you have ever seen the movie *Hoosiers*? It's about a group of young men learning what it means to play the game of basketball as a unit, as a real team. The most interesting part of the whole story comes in observing how the coach gets them to do it—to work as team members who are totally committed to one another. He taught them discipline, hard work, and hustle, to be sure. But the greatest thing he gave them as a coach was the gift of his love. By the end of the season, his hickory hoopsters had forged a bond of love among themselves, and their coach, that went on to fuel a state championship. Ask:

•What is your experience with team building in sports? In other endeavors?
•What would you say are the key ingredients needed in forming a close-knit team that works well together? Do you have examples from family, church, or work place?

After fielding some responses, move to the next portion of your presentation.

THE KEY CONCEPTS

Transition statement: Today, let's think in terms of *us* being a team. Not just our local group, but the whole Body of Christ around the world. We're all on the same team, and we might call this vast team the Kingdom Builders.

But for our small part of the Kingdom, right here, it's my heart's desire that we would grow and become a very tight team—much like the one in the movie. As single adults, we find it easy to plow through life with an individualistic mind-set. However, God has a different plan for our lives. His plan is team, body, community, family, unit. God wants to forge a bond of love among us right here. Let's take a look at His playbook and find out more about this plan.

Read 1 Corinthians 12:31 aloud.

From this Scripture verse we can learn our first Key Concept about building community—

KEY CONCEPT #1:
Love is the most awesome and excellent gift we can give one another.

Tell the group/team about the most awesome gift you have ever received. Then emphasize these three subpoints:

(1) Love is, indeed, a gift. What is the meaning of a gift? Well, for one thing, it can't be demanded; it can only be accepted. A gift is something that flows from the kindness and goodwill of another, out of a gracious heart. A gift comes from one person's joy in the happiness and well-being of another. Naturally, freely given love—unconditional love—is the best thing humans can receive. It is actually what we long for in all of our other endeavors, even though God has already given it to us. We simply need to accept this great gift! As C.S. Lewis said: "God loves us, not because we are loveable but because He is love, not because he needs to receive but because He delights to give."

(2) Love is a gift to be given away and received. Love isn't a possession that we hold on to in order to make ourselves feel good. Some people like to "drop names," telling everyone about who they know and who their friends are. Have you ever done that? In the same way, we can be tempted to take pride in the fact of our being loved or in having someone to love. But this ignores the aspect of love as a gift. It is a giving-and-receiving thing. Actually, we might say that *Love is an action word.* Ask:

•*When have you most clearly and powerfully seen love in action? Why was this event so powerful for you?*

(3) Love is *the most awesome* gift. That's true because of the power of love to transcend hurt, pain, mistrust, bitterness, etc. Our salvation as human beings is based in love. It is therefore the most important and awesome thing we can ever deal with. We may think that we can only survive life's trials if we have enough money, food, security, friends . . . (you name it). But the fact is, people have survived all things, with deep inner peace through the power of love. And it is love that makes it possible for us to survive even death (see I Cor. 15:54-56).

Read the quote from Victor Frankl here (from the Take-Home page).

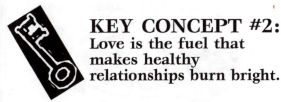

KEY CONCEPT #2:
Love is the fuel that makes healthy relationships burn bright.

Ask someone to read I Peter 3:8 aloud.

From this verse we learn Key Concept #2. Here Peter exhorts the body of believers to be in harmony and to love one another as brothers. The kind of love Peter is talking about is *philadelphos* in the Greek New Testament. The word denotes brotherly and community-type relations. Healthy relationships will take place within

our community when we understand the priority of this kind of love over an erotic love.

Bring in a Coleman lantern, along with some fuel. In front of the group, pour the fuel into the lantern, pump the lantern, and light it. Turn off all the lights, and go through the two points below with just the lantern to light the room.

Stress these points:
(1) All relationships need fuel. But we must constantly ask ourselves: *What is the quality of that fuel?* Some of the "watered down" fuel that people use in relationships might be: lust, sex, power, money, possessions. These things simply fuel co-dependency and form the flimsiest of foundations upon which to build a relationship.

Ask group members to silently consider:

•*Have you ever had a love relationship crash down because of being built on some of these things?*
•*What could you have done differently to build a stronger foundation?*

(2) Biblical love is the best fuel for healthy community. We want our community of believers to be fueled by a dynamic love for Christ, and a healthy brother and sister (*philadelphia* type) love for each other. Some of us have a warped sense of brotherhood-type relationships because of our past experiences. Some of us only see the opposite sex in a romantic way, or as a symbol of the gender that has hurt us deeply. As a result, we find it difficult to experience *philadelphia* with each other.

KEY CONCEPT #3:
Love is the way to influence our world for Christ.

Have someone read John 13:35 aloud.

Say: From this verse we discover our final Key Concept. In John 13:35, Jesus reminds us of the one specific way to change our world. He understood the powerful witness

HINT:

During your mini-lecture, work through the three Key Concepts as a facilitator. Encourage your participants to talk through these points with you; invite questions and/or comments as you go. Offer the concepts and the subpoints, then ask for discussion. Keeping the presentation open-ended in this way allows the group members to focus on their areas of concern— their agenda, rather than yours.

that flows from healthy community when it flourishes in the midst of a hatred-filled world. We want to influence our world for Christ, but we often overlook the best way to do it: our display of mutual love in the Community of Christ. Such a community taps into the deep longings for love carried by every person walking through the doors of our church.

Let's discuss these things for a moment:

• *When have you known of a visitor—a "stranger" in our church who was clearly looking for God's love?*

• *What do you think he or she found here? What are the good aspects of loving community that we seem to have around here?*

• *Where can we strengthen and improve in the depth of mutual love? What practical steps would help?*

Conclusion

Share a personal account of a car accident that you were in or that you witnessed. Or ask a volunteer to tell his or her own crash-story. Talk about the "moment of impact," or the "sound of impact," or "how much damage" the impact caused. Use that story to illustrate that God gives us moments, as a community, to impact our world with love. Ask:

• *If our "team love" had a sound to it, what would it sound like?*

• *How much "good" damage have we caused in this world when it comes to impacting our world with love?*

Our love is an example to all who observe. One of the best ways to influence our world for Christ is when we can lay down our differences and exemplify a powerful love for each other. So consider:

• *How difficult, or easy, is it for you to give up your position (or rights) in an argument or serious conflict with another Christian?*

GOING DEEPER

"Love" in the original Greek. The Greek language of the original New Testament writings has several different words for love. *Eros* denotes intense

physical desire, but neither the verb nor noun form of *eros* exists in the New Testament. The Greek word for a more reciprocal kind of love appears in the Bible a number of times, however. That word is *philos.*

While *eros* is a kind of selfish passion, and *philos* describes a more brotherly love, neither was used consistently by the New Testament writers. The word *agape* [uh-GAH-pay] appears much more frequently. Yet *agape* (unconditional love) describes different expressions of love: the attitude of God toward His Son (John 17:26) and toward the human race generally (John 3:16). It also conveys God's will concerning our attitude one toward another (John 13:34-35), and toward all human beings (1 Thess. 3:12).

One of the main reasons Paul wrote 1 Corinthians 13 was the Corinthian misunderstanding of love. Many of these believers, like some of your singles, didn't comprehend love in any other way but as *eros*. Paul teaches them about a whole new love, a love based on God loving us and us loving others because of that divine love. This is a pure love, a fresh new approach to the way we view and treat others. Paul wanted to draw a line in the sand. He wanted to create a stark contrast between *eros* and *agape* love.

EXTRA OPTIONS

Pick and Choose any of the following to fit the needs of your group...

Options to Consider…for Step 1

Awesome Gift, Charade Style—Do this activity the same as the "Awesome Gift" activity in the Option 1 Opener (on page 10) But when you get to the part about reading the gifts aloud (and trying to figure out who the gifts belong to), have each person act out each one of the gifts for the group. After each charade, the group members can try to figure out who the gifts belong to.

Spot Me!—Have people take partners and explain to everyone that they are going to do what is called "spotting" in various sports (such as rock climbing and trampolining). Safety is important in this activity to insure that no one is hurt.

One person will stand with feet together, rigid body, hands across the chest and eyes closed. The spotter will stand behind this person—who will be falling—and prepare to catch him or her with one foot forward and one back, hands placed at the chosen distance.

The person will fall three times, the first time being only a few inches, the second being a little further, and then finally the third time being a fall of two to three feet (or whatever the participants are comfortable with). Each fall is decided ahead of time so the risk will be known.

Use the commands: "Spotter ready?" followed by "Spotter ready!" and "Falling," followed by "Fall on!" Always maintain safety and don't exceed the level of trust. Discuss:

• *What does it take for you to begin trusting someone in a relationship? How do you know when the other person trusts you deeply?*

• *What role does trust play in "true love"? Can you give an example?*

Lava Crossing—

Needed: An old blanket (8' x 4'), a blindfold, cotton earplugs, and two slings.

Form teams of 6-10 people, then distribute the materials listed above by choosing four different individuals to be blind, deaf, having a broken leg, and having a broken arm. Mark a starting and ending point and inform the team members that they are to traverse an imaginary lava pit by keeping the whole team on the blanket. Give a time limit and encourage teamwork. Discuss the kinds of teamwork required to do this activity.

Water Colors—Divide into groups of six. Provide a feather, a watercolor paint set and two pieces of white construction paper for each group. Let everyone know that their task is to paint a picture starting with the whole feather in one color sweeping across the sheet. Then have everyone in the group take one strand of the feather, with one color each, and draw designs into the one picture. Discuss the elements of teamwork needed in any cooperative endeavor among "big picture" people and detail-oriented folks.

Options to Consider...for Step 3

Measuring Up?—Give each person a ruler, pen, and piece of paper. Have people trace the ruler and mark off every half inch (for 12 inches) on one side of the ruler and every quarter inch on the other side of the ruler. Beside each quarter-inch mark, participants should write the name of a person who has invested love into their lives. Then write the names of each individual they are currently targeting with God's love (or *want* to do so) by the half-inch mark. Follow up with these questions:

•How do you measure up? Are you receiving more love than you give? Or vice versa?
•In what ways could you improve your love-giving measurement?

Love Pictures x 2—Split the group up into teams of four. Have team members draw two pictures. One of the kind of love that Paul is talking about in 1 Corinthians 13, and one of the kind of love that is present in their singles group. Note: They cannot use any words in their pictures! After the time allotted, invite participants to share their pictures with the entire group—and explain them.

Lasting Impressions—Have everyone sit back-to-back with a partner. Then ask partners to interview one another to find out as many details about their lives as possible, in these areas: work, family, relationships, personal struggles. Finally, have the partners write out one another's prayer needs and spend some time interceding for one another. Ask for ongoing prayer commitments during the week ahead.

Options to Consider...for Step 4

Give It Away—Brainstorm for practical ways to show unconditional love—toward other group members and toward "outsiders." List all ideas on a chalkboard or newsprint, then gather resources and decide to implement the Top Five ideas. These might include such things as: sending notes of appreciation, doing yard work, bringing dessert to a grieving family, washing someone's car for free...Be creative!

Did You Hear That?—Have four people sit back to back, and allow these folks one minute each to engage in "good gossip" (that is, they will tell how awesome they think the person sitting behind them is). Each person speaks only about the person backing up to them. After the minute is up, switch to the other person. After two minutes, say: "Now turn all your chairs inwards and share what you heard about yourself."

Accountability Calls—Make plans to prepare a phone calling network for prayer and accountability. On the list beside each person's name would be the accountability question they want to have asked to them during the middle of each week.

Options to Consider...for Step 5

Chocolate Greetings—Bring a bag of Hershey Kisses to your session. At the close of your time together, make the bags available for people to grab a Kiss and give it to someone. Let everyone know that they'll be representing the biblical command to, "Greet one another with a holy kiss."

Partnership Prayers—Have everyone sit on the floor facing one another and holding hands. This teaches people to have sincere love for one another as they pray together.

BIBLE TEXT

WHADDAYA THINK?

- In your opinion, what is the strongest evidence for Christianity in our world today? Why? How have you seen this work?
- Why is it important to demonstrate our love for one another as Christians? In what ways is the love within the Christian community like, and unlike, other kinds of love?
- What kinds of interpersonal involvement are required to develop strong bonds of love in the church?
- If you were to rate the level of our group's mutual love, would it be:

____ a huge, overflowing, gushing, cascading, soaking river of affection?
____ a nice little waterfall, splashing on a few tourists?
____ a serene, peaceful pond in the wilderness, unknown to most campers?
____ a tiny underground current beneath some tough bedrock?
____ a dried-up desert stream?

- If improvement is needed, what would you suggest?

KEY CONCEPTS
on Excellent Love

#1 Love is the most_____
and_____
gift we can_____.
#2 Love is the _____that makes healthy
relationships _____.
#3 Love is the way to _____
for Christ.

LOVE DIVIDED

Draw a circular pie-chart of your activities, showing how you spend your typical day. The chart should indicate ratios of time—including the percentage of "love energy" you use most days. With arrows, state where this energy goes. Consider, and share:

- *How would I like to redraw my chart, if I could?*
- *What practical things could I do to make giving and receiving love a greater priority in my daily life?*

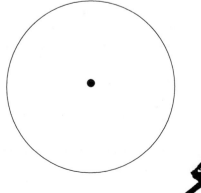

But eagerly desire the greater gifts. And now I will show you the most excellent way.
—1 Corinthians 12:31

Finally, all of you, live in harmony with one another; be sympathetic, love as brothers, be compassionate and humble.
—1 Peter 3:8

A new command I give you: Love one another. As I have loved you, so you must love one another. By this all men will know that you are my disciples, if you love one another.
—John 13:34-35

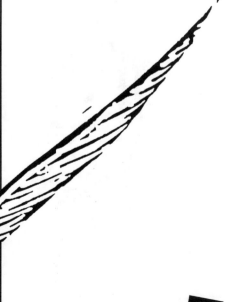

But eagerly desire the greater gifts. And now I will show you the most excellent way.
—1 Corinthians 12:31

Finally, all of you, live in harmony with one another; be sympathetic, love as brothers, be compassionate and humble.
—1 Peter 3:8

A new command I give you: Love one another. As I have loved you, so you must love one another. By this all men will know that you are my disciples, if you love one another.
—John 13:34-35

AGREE OR DISAGREE?

Respond to these statements by stating your agreement or disagreement:
1. Effort and human motivation are not enough when it comes to finding love.
2. God's love is only available through a relationship with Jesus Christ.
3. Obedience must always prevail over feelings and emotions.
4. Love never fails, ever!

KEY CONCEPTS
on Excellent Love

#1 Love is the most _____ and
_____ gift we can
_____.

#2 Love is the _____ that makes healthy relationships
_____ _____.

#3 Love is the_____for Christ.

LETTING GO

To let go doesn't mean to stop caring, it means I can't do it for someone else.

To let go is not to cut myself off, it's the realization that I don't control another.

To let go is not to enable, but to allow learning from natural consequences.

To let go is to admit powerlessness, which means the outcome is not in my hands.

To let go is not to try to change or blame another, I can only change myself.

To let go is not to care for, but to care about.

To let go is not to fix, but to be supportive.

To let go is not to judge, but to allow another to be a human being.

To let go is not to be in the middle arranging all the outcomes, but to allow others to affect their own outcomes.

To let go is not to be protective, it is to permit another to face reality.

To let go is not to deny but to accept.

To let go is not to nag, scold, or argue, but to search out my own shortcomings and to correct them.

To let go is not to adjust everything to my desires but to take each day as it comes and to cherish the moment.

To let go is not to criticize and regulate anyone but to try to become what I dream I can be.

To let go is not to regret the past but to grow and live for the future.

To let go is to fear less and love more. —Author Unknown

For the first time in my life I saw the truth as it is set into song by so many poets, proclaimed as the final wisdom by so many thinkers. The truth—that love is the ultimate and the highest goal to which man can aspire. Then I grasped the meaning of the greatest secret that human poetry and human thought and belief have to impart: The salvation of man is through love and in love. I understood how a man who has nothing left in this world still may know bliss, be it only for a brief moment, in the contemplation of his beloved. In a position of utter desolation, when man cannot express himself in positive action, when his only achievement may consist in enduring his sufferings in the right way—an honorable way—in such a position man can, through loving contemplation of the image he carries of his beloved, achieve

(CONTINUES FLIPSIDE)

Take Home Page MARCH

TIME FOR A RESPONSE

The most personally relevant thing I've learned in this session is:

How can I apply the three Key Concepts?

In my friendships:

In my church/personal ministry:

In my community:

In my workplace:

As a single parent (teaching this principle to my kids):

With my roommate(s):

THE NEXT STEP
(Projects and Ideas for the Week Ahead)

1. Divorced Singles: Help out with the hospitality needs of people in your church. Help prepare meals for the sick, the pregnant, or a new family in the community.

2. Generation Xers: Put together a "Senior Citizens Prom." Make it extend over the whole weekend, with a picnic, formal dinner, and entertainment. Offer pictures and everything!

3. Older Singles: Ask a date to the Prom! (See above.)

4. Single Parents: Go ice skating or roller skating with your kids. Treat the event like a date and get them flowers, candy, and a card expressing your love for them. Don't do it for their birthday; they expect it then. Surprise them, and use the occasion to teach your children how to give their love in practical ways.

Take Home Page HABIT
continued

DAILY READINGS AND REFLECTIONS

Monday — Read 1 Corinthians 13:4 and Romans 5:5. What is the source of unending love? Think: Is it in our power or nature to be loving?

Tuesday — Read 2 Peter 1 and 2 Peter 3:9. What has God done to exhibit love to us? How can we practice this love?

Wednesday — Read John 13:34-35. How does a true disciple follow Jesus? How are you, personally, responding to Christ's call?

Thursday — Read Matthew 5:38-48. How should we treat those we hold little affection for?

Friday — Read 2 Peter 1:5. Do you act immediately in faith when it comes to loving others? What is your typical response?

Saturday — Read Romans 8:27, 34. How often do you find "strangers" in your life to intercede for?

RANKING LOVE

Rank these acts of love, assigning each a number between 1 and 10 (1 being the greatest act of love possible). Then answer the discussion questions that follow.

___ A father cheering for his son at a Little League baseball game.

___ Steve holding his girlfriend's hand as he proposes marriage.

___ An army nurse comforting a soldier who has just had his legs amputated.

___ A woman sitting across from her rapist at a prison, offering forgiveness to him.

___ A hostage on an airliner jumping in front of a bullet meant for another person.

___ Mrs. Smith signing the paper to release her son's organs after he died in a car accident.

___ Greg jumping into raging flood waters to save a screaming child.

___ Grandpa kissing Grandma before bedtime.

___ Captain John Thomas flying his third mission for the United States Air Force.

___ Mrs. Larson teaching about Jonah in the second-grade Sunday school classroom where she has taught for the last 35 years.

- **To what extent can acts of love be put on a scale?**
- **Do we as Christians tend to pursue doing the "greater" acts of love? Explain.**
- **What acts of love seem to separate Christians from the world?**
- **Can a group accomplish acts of love? How? What might some of those be?**

FINISH THE THOUGHT...

- When it comes to understanding love as a gift, I give love best by . . . .

- I like people to show me love by . . . .

SAY THE WORDS

Many of us find it quite difficult to share words of love. And that's too bad, because saying the actual words — "I love you" — is so powerful. Name five people in your life that you will commit to saying "I love you" to — face to face:

1.

2.

3.

4.

5.

Session 2
A Deepening
DEVOTION

SESSION AIM

To help single adults deepen their devotion to basic spiritual commitments—the things that built community in the early church.

"My life is so complicated right now," Juanita moaned. **"With everything coming at me so fast, I feel like I'm in a shooting gallery—and I'm the target!"**

Look out! What's going to hit you next?

Most single adults can relate to the daily challenge of dodging the success-threatening missles speeding their way. Every day we're confronted with myriad demands and choices that drain our time and energy. Just keeping up with basic responsibilities can require significant concentration and unflagging effort.

Unfortunately, life can get so crazy that we easily overlook the most foundational spiritual commitments. Yet, when we look at the believers in the early church, we see them experiencing powerful community and profound spiritual life change. All because of the "uncomplicated" commitments to which they had devoted themselves.

This session is about teaching your adults to be devoted to those same things—with unflinching singlemindedness. In Acts 2:42-47, thousands of people responded to the apostle Peter's preaching. These new believers immediately set their sails for a new course in life. They stripped themselves of all previous commitments and became a dynamic community that made an impact for God.

Perhaps we're making our lives more difficult than they need to be. Isn't there an undeniable potency in simplifying, downsizing, and prioritizing what is important? No doubt God wants to help us set our sails on a new course, too. It begins with a renewed devotion to the things that really matter.

WHAT'S IT ALL ABOUT?

Keep these Key Concepts in mind as you move through each step of your lesson: The early believers made four specific commitments in their lives—

• They devoted themselves to truth—knowing it and spreading it.
• They committed their time and efforts to a team of believers.
• They gave themselves whole-heartedly to a corporate prayer life.
• They pooled their resources as a team—in order to give, give, give.

BIBLE REFERENCES:

Acts 2:42-47
Romans 12:9-13

23

1—Let's Get Started
(5-10 minutes)

Option 1: Lead Me On
Needed: Rope and tennis balls, or objects that can be stepped on without causing injury.

In advance, lay out an obstacle course using the balls and rope. Then form groups of six to eight people and tell everyone that their task is to lead a "blind" member through the obstacle course. A blindfolded person from each group will walk through the obstacle course with the aid of his or her team—who give these basic verbal instructions only: "forward," "back," "right," "left." The instructors must take turns saying one of these words. Have teams compete by deducting points for every touch of an obstacle. Ask:

•*When have you found it better to stick with basic instructions, rather than explaining complicated procedures?*
•*In your opinion, is spiritual growth a "basic thing" or a "complicated thing"?*

Option 2: Have You Ever?
Form a large circle. Tell the group that you are going to call out a series of questions. If they have ever done what is mentioned, individuals should run into the middle of the circle and give everyone else who has done this thing a "High Five."

Make up your own wacky questions, for example: Have you ever . . . been out of the country, been to the opera, asked for directions after being lost for two hours, laughed so hard you couldn't breath, hiccuped and burped at the same time, gotten a "D" in school, etc. . . . Follow up with this final question for brief discussion:

•*Have you ever been so devoted to a accomplishing a task with others that it caused you to grow very close to one another? Tell about that experience.*

Option 3: Discussion
Use the "Choice Position" exercise on Interactive Page #1.

2—Looking to the Word
(15 minutes)

Present the material found in "Presenting What the Bible Has to Say," on pages 28-30. Divide your time between the three segments: Introduction, Key Concepts, and Conclusion.

3—Applying It to My Life
(5-10 minutes)

As soon as you complete your presentation, move into small groups and have the youngest person lead the discussion by asking the questions from "Whaddaya Think?" on the Interactive page #1.

4—Taking the Next Step
(5 minutes)

In advance, call the pastor or an elder of your church and ask if there are any jobs which really need doing in the church. Find out how the singles could help. Then, after your group has worked on the "Meals on Feet" section of Interactive Page #1, give them the list of things that need to be done. Ask for volunteers—and a specific commitment of time and effort.

5—Let's Wrap It Up
(5 minutes)

1. Move into small groups of two or three people and offer a time for each person to share some of the most awesome answers-to-prayer stories in their life. Discuss what issues were at the heart of the situation. Then choose a common prayer request and focus on this in corporate prayer.

2. Make your group's announcements at this time, and then distribute the Take Home Page.

HINT:
You may wish to make some preliminary comments about "devotion" in general, before your mini-lecture. Here's two ideas. Look up the psychology of how a dog devotes himself to his owner or:

•Illustrate with your dog—or someone else's—who is well behaved and loves his owner.
•Bring out the characteristics of a dog that make him "man's best friend."
•See if you can find a few "Rescue Stories" that tell about a dog saving her owner.

When You Have More Time...

(How to Use This Material in 60-90 Minutes)

Example: Small Groups at Home

1—Let's Get Started
(5-10 minutes)

Option 1: Team-working Channels
Needed: A strip of construction paper for each person, one marble for each group, and one paper cup for each group.

Form a long line and give each person a 1" x 12" strip of construction paper. Fold the strip in half, lengthwise. Explain to the group members that they will be given a marble and must create a channel for the marble to travel from the starting point into a paper cup at the finish point. Specify that the channels can only move up or down, not sideways, and they must make contact with one another when the marble is transferred. Work together to make it work! Let everyone know that "a good team"—one that can really concentrate—should be able to do it in about five tries. Then discuss:

•*What things do you concentrate on most—to make your life flow smoothly along?*

Option 2: Skit Development
Begin your session with the "Skit With a Purpose" activity on Interactive Page #2. Be sure to have volunteers perform the finished production!

Option 3: Discussion
Use the questions on Interactive Page #2, under "Interact #1." Have small groups discuss their responses and then report to the large group.

2—Looking to the Word
(20-25 minutes)

Present the material found in "Presenting What the Bible Has to Say," on pages 28-30. Divide your allotted time into three segments: (1) Introduction, (2) Key Concepts, and (3) Conclusion. Keep your presentation short and simple. Hit the highlights, drawing upon the "Going Deeper" information as appropriate.

3—Applying It to My Life
(20-25 minutes)

As soon as you complete your presentation, have everyone read the story under "Interact #2" on Interactive Page #2. Then, in buzz groups, answer the questions below the story.

4—Taking the Next Step
(10-20 minutes)

1. Make your group's announcements at this time.
2. Distribute the Take Home Page. Allow a period of silence for individuals to work through the "Time for a Response" section by jotting answers. Ask volunteers to share a bit about their responses before moving to step five.

5—Let's Wrap It Up
(5 minutes)

Needed: Slips of paper; a "hat" or small box/bowl.

1. Have each individual draw a word out of a hat and brainstorm with the group for practical actions (representing each word) that they could do in the week ahead. Use words related to today's session, such as: fellowship, team, commitment, prayer, give, truth, time, energy, praising, hospitable, and patient.
2. Decide on one action to take, and close in prayer for God's help in carrying it out.

HINT:
To create a sense of continuity throughout this course, briefly review the Key Concepts from the previous week's session. Today, ask your singles how they attempted to give away their gift of love during the past week. Also, remind everyone that this lesson is about the "basics," including things they may have heard before. However, encourage group members to "think new" about today's foundational principles for living and growing in community.

Extending The Learning...
(How to Use This Material in Two Hours)
Example: Extended Week-Night Program

1—Let's Get Started
(20-30 minutes)

Option 1: Yarn It!
Needed: Numerous lengths of yarn (cut into 1-foot sections); a box of straws for each pair.

Have partners attempt to build a structure with yarn and straws. Challenge them to build the largest structure possible, with these stipulations: no two straws or pieces of yarn can touch each other. (You might also limit the pieces of yarn available to each pair.) After judging the architectural masterpieces, discuss:

•*When have you felt that your commitment to a task or cause was flimsy and could crumble at any moment? What happened?*

Option 2: Human Knot
In groups of 6 to 10, sit down in a circle. Have each person reach out his or her right hand across the circle to another person's right hand. Then reach out the left hand and grab a different person's left hand. Keep holding hands and begin to untie the knot your group is in. Make this rule: the hands may rotate but may not disconnect! The object is to end up with a complete circle when you are done. Then discuss:

•*On a scale of 1 to 10, how much concentration would you say was required to untie ourselves? How much concentration does it take you to solve your daily problems? To stay strong and committed to Jesus Christ? To grow in your fellowship with others in this group?*

Option 3: Quote Reactions
Distribute the Take Home Page and direct everyone's attention to the "In Other Words" section. Assign half the group to read and meditate on the first quotation, and half the group to do the same with the second quotation. After a few minutes ask:

•*What is your initial reaction to this quotation? In what ways is it relevant to your life right now?*

2—Looking to the Word
(20 minutes)

Offer a brief mini-lecture using the material found in "Presenting What the Bible Has to Say," on pages 28-30.

3—Applying It to My Life
(30-40 minutes)
Needed: Pencils or pens.

Once you've presented your mini-lecture, use the "Pool Your Resources!" exercise on the Take Home Page. First give each individual a chance to fill in their "pools." Then ask the group to work together (perhaps brainstorming) to decide how the team can put these resources together to corporately invest in other people (in the group, the church, or the community at large). Push for specific strategies.

4—Taking the Next Step
(30-40 minutes)
Needed: Paper and pencils.

Begin by having individuals find a quiet place in the building (or outside) in order to spend 10 minutes alone in prayer. People should ask for God to work through them as they attempt to apply today's Key Concepts in practical ways. Then they should list the things in their lives that need to be stripped away to allow for a deeper devotion to the basic commitments they've learned about.
Finally, if participants seem open to it, form pairs and suggest significant vulnerability in talking through this topic (jot on chalkboard or newsprint): "The things that seem to be hindering me from devoting my whole life to Christ."

5—Let's Wrap It Up
(5-10 minutes)

Make your group's announcements and close in prayer.

My Personal Game Plan

STEP 1   Time: _____ minutes.

Materials Needed:

Activities Summary:

STEP 2   Time: _____ minutes.

Materials Needed:

Activities Summary:

STEP 3   Time: _____ minutes.

Materials Needed:

Activities Summary:

STEP 4   Time: _____ minutes.

Materials Needed:

Activities Summary:

STEP 5   Time: _____ minutes.

Materials Needed:

Activities Summary:

Just for You
Teacher's Devotional

As leaders, we may find it easy to get caught up in preparing learning experiences for others. But what are we, ourselves, learning? When we enter into God's Word, do we constantly end up saying to ourselves, *Oh...this would be so good for my singles group to hear...?* If so, we're robbing ourselves of the blessing God's Word can have on us.

Remember: As you go, your singles go. Another way to say it: You will never take your singles farther in the spiritual life than where you are right now!

On the scale below, rank yourself as to where you think you are spiritually this week:

5_____   I've finally reached complete spiritual maturity. I should be

4_____   whisked away to heaven at any moment.

3_____

2_____   My devotion is all dried up. I'm in a barren desert

1_____   dying, crying out for the waters of spiritual Life.

Jot down some ideas about how you might be able to move one step further along the line to maturity before leading your next singles group session. Keeping in mind, of course, that all spiritual growth is ultimately the result of pure, unconditional grace. Depend upon Him—and God's blessings upon you and your group this week!

—Joel and Kent

- TO HELP SINGLE ADULTS

_____
_____
_____

- TO HELP SINGLE ADULTS

_____
_____
_____

- TO HELP SINGLE ADULTS

_____
_____
_____

- TO HELP SINGLE ADULTS

_____
_____
_____

WHAT I LEARNED FROM READING 'LOOKING TO THE WORD' . . .

Notes and Insights—

27

Presenting
What the Bible Has to Say...

Here's your mini-lecture covering the biblical Key Concepts. Try to become familiar with the flow of thoughts, and the outline, in order to present this material with maximum eye contact. Special instructions to you are in bold type. (Note: Have group members refer to the Key Concepts section on their Interactive Page. They may wish to fill in the blanks as you speak.)

Introduction

Begin by showing your group three pictures (which you have drawn with a crayon) of things that you were "devoted to" when you were twelve years old. Some examples might be: a favorite bike, Mom and Dad, friends across the street, a favorite doll, etc.

After you've shown those pictures and talked about them a bit, show three current pictures (Polaroids, if possible, or drawings) of the things that you are devoted to now. Bring out the differences between the two time periods and the two "you"s. Especially draw attention to how you (hopefully) have progressed in the things that you are committing your time and energies to today. Talk about the importance of growth, change, and maturity in the things to which you are now devoting your life.

In these next few moments, I'd like to challenge each of you with the concept of deeper devotion. I'd like you to take an inventory concerning the things in your life to which you are devoting your time and resources. And I'd like you to join me on an exploration of the early church Christians—to observe what they devoted themselves to.

As you know, the early Christians were a unique group of people that made a powerful impact on their world. They were the true personification of team and family! I believe they experienced personal spiritual growth and "glue-like" community because *they made at least four specific commitments in their lives.* Let's take a look at those things.

Read Acts 2:42:47 aloud in front of the group.

KEY CONCEPT #1:
They devoted themselves to truth—knowing it and spreading it.

Illustration. When a pilot flys in fog or at night, she must be totally committed to using her navigational instruments. These instruments are the required tools for making it through the fog and darkness. Without them, a crash could easily occur, and she would never reach her destination. How is biblical truth like a pilot's instruments? Consider:

Make these Subpoints—

(1) The truth orients our lives. Have you noticed that life can be like flying through a fog?Ask:

• *When has it been the foggiest for you?*
• *What situations make it tough for you to get your bearings—emotionally and spiritually?*

Yes, we can find ourselves surrounded by darkness. The truth always proves to be the instrument we need in order to make it through life. That's because it is the most crucial thing to have in order to make good decisions.

(2) The truth requires unusual commitment. Because of the pressures of life, we must have more than an "average" or "normal" commitment to the Scriptures. Actually, we must go overboard, be unusually diligent in our approach to the truth and its role in our daily decisions. Just worshiping on Sunday mornings, or spending the occasional quiet time in the Word really won't get it!

(3) The truth is for individual use. We have to use the truth in practical ways if it is to help us navigate through life. In order to experience community, we must experience the power of God's Word—personally. It's important that each of us has a vibrant, growing relationship with Jesus. That's the case because we must be able to offer each other Christ, and His truth, for our relationships here to flourish. That can't happen unless we have something to give.

KEY CONCEPT #2:
They committed their time and efforts to a team of believers.

Illustration. **Prepare ahead of time to make this point: Talk is cheap! Have someone in the group stand up and share a need that they have right now (for example: need a brake job on their car, need to do household chores, need to find a baby-sitter, etc.). Tell the group that you would like to pray for that need. Have the person sit down, and say to the group:**

While it is crucial to pray for one another's needs, we must combine our prayers with direct actions that help. Before I pray, is there anyone here who can meet this need with their personal resources? **(If no one responds, then pray.)**

Now emphasize these points:

(1) Genuine love demands action. We can come to church, and we can pray, but we need to go about loving each other enough to take action. The Christian life is lived out within the time and tangible energies that we offer to each other.

(2) Mutual love is a double blessing. When we give our time and energies, we produce a double blessing. That is, God encourages the person that we are giving to, and He also encourages and facilitates our own spiritual growth as we give.

Have someone read aloud Matthew 14:23-24.

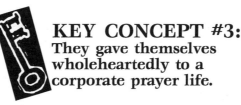

KEY CONCEPT #3:
They gave themselves wholeheartedly to a corporate prayer life.

In this passage, Jesus talks about the importance of praying alone. Yet, while praying alone is critical to spiritual success, praying together with a team of believers is just as critical to our spiritual growth. Why? Consider these two practical reasons:

(1) Corporate prayer keeps us in touch with need. It announces to God, others, and ourselves that we are NEEDY. Admitting need is what God loves to hear from His children. It "allows" Him to be strong and us to be weak (which is how things really are)! Corporate prayer brings about a certain spiritual awareness of others and their needs.

(2) Corporate prayer increases our love and fellowship. It acts as a "bonding agent" that produces team unity. As singles we must constantly guard against becoming "single" focused. It's too easy for us to become independent followers of God. Corporate prayer allows us to be "other" focused and *inter*dependent followers of Christ.

KEY CONCEPT #4:
They pooled their resources as a team— in order to give, give, give.

Illustration. There are things in my basement (or garage, attic) that I have stored in order to use one day for a certain purpose. Things like these. See if you can guess what these items are. **(Choose two or three unusual items that would be fairly difficult for the group to recognize. After a few guesses, explain what the items are and how you use them.)**

In our lives we all have "basements." And we have things—resources—stored there that can be be used for a certain purpose. We are called to identify these resources, and then "give them away" for God's glory.

The point is: The early believers kept on giving. These Christians enjoyed great

HINT:

Teacher's Tip
Make every effort to be a visual teacher. Your singles will remember the visuals you use to illustrate your points because visuals involve more of the senses. Be an impact teacher, work toward teaching your singles with things that will last and change lives.

community. Much of this was because they unselfishly gave, gave, and gave to each other. They left nothing on the basement shelves of their lives. They were consumed with meeting each others' needs by pooling their resources. That is what our community here needs to be doing. We need to pull things off the shelves and give to each other. This is one of the greatest ways of demonstrating the reality of Jesus Christ today. Ask:

•*Silently consider: What are some things in your "basement" that you could pull off the shelf and give to someone else for God's glory?*

Conclusion

David Livingstone once said, "People talk of the sacrifice I have made in spending so much of my life in Africa. Can that be called a sacrifice which is simply paid back as a small part of a great debt owed to our God, which we can never repay?"

David Livingstone was a man of devotion.

He understood that his time spent in Africa was nothing more than his opportunity to give back to God. In the same way, the things that you devote your life to offer unique opportunities to give back to God. For He has given us so much. We can devote the sweat of our lives to so many empty pursuits. But there are none more important or crucial than the truths we have talked about today.

Think about it: Devoting ourselves to the truth, committing our time to a team of believers, giving ourselves to corporate prayer, and pooling our resources—all are eternal pursuits. It's the kind of stuff that must make God smile.

GOING DEEPER

Fellowship word study. Here are three Greek New Testament words related to the English word "fellowship"—

Koinonia [koi-noe-NEE-ah]. From the word *koinos,* meaning "common." Synonyms: communion, fellowship, sharing. See 1 Corinthians 10:16.

Metoche **[met-oh-KAY]**. Means "partnership." See 2 Corinthians 6:14.

Koinonos **[koy-NAH-nahs]**. Denotes a "partaker" or "partner." See 1 Corinthians 10:20.

Some background on the Christians of Acts 2. Many of the three thousand baptized people (see vs. 41) had been eyewitnesses to the death of Christ. One of the interesting things about this group is that they accepted the Gospel message with such interest and openness. While kings, rulers, and leaders in the Bible heard the message of God's Word, many failed to receive the message as these early believers did.

After they became baptized, most of these new Christians apparently enrolled in a discipleship program. They got busy with the work of following Christ, starting out as infants and growing to maturity as a unit. Lloyd Ogilvie says, "Next to the transformation of persons, the second greatest miracle is oneness with others who have been transformed." The early Christians experienced such oneness. They grew each day in Christian solidarity as the world looked on. They became, and were, the church. Their desires were simple, and as a result, the message was not blurred. It was perfectly clear to the world around them.

EXTRA OPTIONS

Pick and Choose any of the following to fit the needs of your group...

Options to Consider...for Step 1

Weird Olympics—Invite your extroverts to show their devotion to winning—in weird ways—for the enjoyment of all. Get them to compete in front of everyone at the following:

1. See who can pick up the most Fruit Loops on a toothpick while it is held in the mouth. No assistance in any way!

2. See who'll be first to finish a whole jar of baby food with a straw. (Choose the "good flavors.")

3. See who can stuff the most crackers in his or her mouth—and still be able to whistle "Yankee Doodle."

4. Judge who has made the funniest face with an orange peel in the mouth.

5. Who can hold the most grapes between their lips, without using the tongue.

Think of a few of your own weird events. This is a great crowd breaker for newcomers, too.

Lean On—Illustrate "team trust"—that the whole team can support each individual leaning in or out. Have your group members stand in a circle and hold hands at the wrist. Spread out so there is only a slight drop in the arms below the shoulders. Number off around the circle, and then explain that on the count of three, the odd numbers will lean in and the even numbers will lean back. (There must be an even number of participants, so you will be either involved or not.) After the

first success, tell everyone to switch on the count of three.

Wink 'Em Icebreaker—Have half of the group sit in a circle on chairs, while the other half stands behind the chairs with their hands behind their backs and looking directly down at the others' shoulders. One standing person starts with an empty chair. The object of the game is for the "standers" to keep the "sitters" in their chairs by grabbing their shoulders and stopping them from getting away if they respond to a wink. The person with the empty chair must try to get someone to come to her chair by winking at them.

Options to Consider...for Step 3

Blind Walk Trust-Building—Have everyone join a group of three. Instruct one person to shut her eyes and extend her hands forward facing down. Have the other two people go to the person, one on each side, with their hands underneath the middle person's hands.

The object of the activity is for the outside people to guide the person in the middle around the room or area. The hands movements are the only "directions" given. If the person is to move forward, the guides simply begin walking. If they want the person to step up, then they raise their hands. This is a major trust activity, and therefore safety must be all-important. As always, stress: no joking around.

While walking the person, the two on the outside ask questions of the one in the middle. Challenge them to ask some deep questions as well as fun ones.

Here are some samples:

- *Tell about one of your most embarrassing moments.*
- *Describe your first kiss on a date.*
- *How long have you been a Christian?*
- *When was the greatest time in your relationship with Christ?*
- *What is He doing in your life now?*

Goal Cutouts—From newspapers or magazines, cut out various words or phrases to display the goal statements for your group. Tape them on poster board to represent your team's interpretation of the lesson and how it could be applied to your lives.

Options to Consider...for Step 4

Cup of Life—Give each person a disposable Cup and take turns having people describe themselves with reference to the cup. Tell group members that this will be a significant way to determine how they can be committed to their team. Each person is to explain how the cup resembles their team and their relationship to it. For example: Do they sense that they need to "pour more into this group," or "take more in from the group"? When everyone has responded briefly, ask for more detailed explanations.

Apply it Outside—During step four, everybody head outdoors! Go to a nearby playground or beach in a small group and play with some of the local kids. Perhaps ask parents first, letting them know who you are and what you are doing.
 Or: Go to a local grocery store and carry bags to cars for people. Check with the store manager first. Enjoy serving others, and take nothing in return except the joy of serving.

Options to Consider...for Step 5

"I Do"—Form small groups and give each group a rose. Have each person pull off a petal and tell how they will commit time and energy to the group during the week. Then end by explaining the real beauty of a rose: it occurs when *all the petals are together in full bloom.* It takes each person to commit to this group to make it as beautiful as Christ wants it to be.

Help Number—Ask for volunteers to be part of a "911 Team" for the church. Then advertise a "Help Number" that people in the church can call if they'd like a single person to help them with anything. If possible, use one person's pager; then someone on a list can be notified to help.

Taped Reinforcement—Hand out an audio-taped message of your favorite speaker. Ask your singles to listen to the tape at least twice this next week. Tell them that, as opposed to turning on the radio to or from work, they could listen to the tape. Ask them to make some journal notes about how the tape affects their attitude during the day.

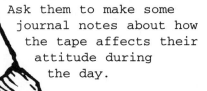

Interactive Page 1

WHADDAYA THINK?

- What do you think of when you hear "be devoted to one another"?
- What are some of the things you are unusually devoted to in your life?
- What do you think Jesus was totally devoted to?
- In what practical ways can we increase our devotion to Christ and the church?
- What do you think it means to have "everything in common"?
- What has been your most satisfying experience with corporate prayer?

CHOICE POSITION

Share your response in small groups:

If you were on a football team, what position would you likely play?
Quarterback (Leader), fullback (blocker), receiver (problem solver), line (defender), defensive line (doer), linebacker (coordinator), defensive back (planner), punter (dependable), coach (Organizer/Motivator), trainer (caregiver), or cheerleader (encourager).

- ***Explain your response by telling about a real-life "play" you made (i.e., how you've been a coordinator, a motivator, an encourager, etc., in a particular situation).***

KEY CONCEPTS
on Deepening Devotion

The early believers made four specific commitments in their lives—

#1 They devoted themselves to _____—_____ing it and _____ing it.

#2 They committed their _____ and _____ to a _____ of believers.

#3 They gave themselves wholeheartedly to a _____ life.

#4 They _____ their _____ as a team—in order to give, give, give.

MEALS ON FEET

Read Acts 6:1-7 and respond:

- How serious was the problem?

- Who initiated the solution?

- Who was given the job? Why?

- What are some jobs in your church or group that are not getting done?

- Who could do them?

They devoted themselves to the apostles' teaching and to the fellowship, to the breaking of bread and to prayer. 43 Everyone was filled with awe, and many wonders and miraculous signs were done by the apostles. 44 All the believers were together and had everything in common. 45 Selling their possessions and goods, they gave to anyone as he had need. 46 Every day they continued to meet together in the temple courts. They broke bread in their homes and ate together with glad and sincere hearts, 47 praising God and enjoying the favor of all the people. And the Lord added to their number daily those who were being saved.
—Acts 2:42-47

Love must be sincere. Hate what is evil; cling to what is good. 10 Be devoted to one another in brotherly love. Honor one another above yourselves. 11 Never be lacking in zeal, but keep your spiritual fervor, serving the Lord. 12 Be joyful in hope, patient in affliction, faithful in prayer. 13 Share with God's people who are in need. Practice hospitality.
—Romans 12:9-13

33

They devoted them-selves to the apostles' teaching and to the fellowship, to the breaking of bread and to prayer. ⁴³ Everyone was filled with awe, and many wonders and miraculous signs were done by the apostles. ⁴⁴ All the believers were together and had everything in common. ⁴⁵ Selling their possessions and goods, they gave to anyone as he had need. ⁴⁶ Every day they continued to meet together in the temple courts. They broke bread in their homes and ate together with glad and sincere hearts, ⁴⁷ praising God and enjoying the favor of all the people. And the Lord added to their number daily those who were being saved.
—Acts 2:42-47

Love must be sincere. Hate what is evil; cling to what is good. ¹⁰ Be devoted to one another in brotherly love. Honor one another above yourselves. ¹¹ Never be lacking in zeal, but keep your spiritual fervor, serving the Lord. 12 Be joyful in hope, patient in affliction, faithful in prayer. ¹³ Share with God's people who are in need. Practice hospitality.
—Romans 12:9-13

SKIT WITH A PURPOSE

Scenario: The youth pastor at your church needs a skit that will help teach the students about "devotion" and how it applies to building community. Many of the students are leaving youth group for other things like work, sports, and school work. Think of a skit that could teach the principle of devotion to these young people.

Notes:

Interact #1

Remember junior-high gym class? When it came time to pick teams and you wanted more than anything to be picked first because you wanted to win?

Being on a team is one of the greatest feelings in the world, especially when it is a winning team. As Christians, we also need to be on a team and have the goal of winning. In order to do this, we must surround ourselves with people who have our best interest at heart.

•*If you were picking a team to help you grow in Christ, what kind of people would you want on your team? What would their part be in your life? What would be your role in their lives?*

Interact #2

As the story goes... A small group of Russian Christians gathered together for a Bible study one evening during World War II when the SS knocked on the door and demanded, "Are there any Christians in this house?"

The soldiers stated that if anyone denied being a Christian they could leave immediately. One person crumbled and said "I am not!" and fearfully hurried out the door. The rest remained, expecting to be shot for their beliefs.

But then one of the soldiers shut the door and approached the middle of the group, saying, "Do not be frightened, we are also Christians, and we would like to fellowship with you. But we had to make sure you were what you said you were."

•*How would your group compare to this group?*
•*How can we improve in our courage and unity? What would this look like, in practical, everyday terms?*

KEY CONCEPTS
on Deepening Devotion

The early believers made four specific commitments in their lives—

#1 They devoted themselves to _____ — _____ing it and _____ing it.

#2 They committed their _____ and _____ to a _____ of believers.

#3 They gave themselves wholeheartedly to a _____ life.

#4 They _____ their _____ as a team—in order to give, give, give.

Take Home Page

TIME FOR A RESPONSE

The most personally relevant thing I've learned in this session is:

[ ]

• What would it mean for me to be totally devoted to truth in my life?

I would have to_____.

I would need to_____.

• What would it mean for me to commit my time and energies to my group or team?

I could spend my time by_____.

I could expend my energies in_____.

•What would it mean for me to commit myself to corporate prayer?

I would pray with_____for _____ times a month. (Jot the names of at least three team members.)

I would need to recruit_____ to be on my prayer team. (Jot down names of some possibilities.)

POOL YOUR RESOURCES!

What are some of your personal resources—things stored in your "basement" of gifts and talents—that you could throw into the pool? (Draw a swimming pool below, and then float a few pictures in it that depict what you have to offer your group.)

TAKE IT TO THE STREETS

Interview someone outside of your singles group, who is also single, and ask him or her these questions:

1. What was the greatest team you were a member of?

2. What were the advantages of being on that team?

3. What should a team do for each of its players?

4. Do people need to feel that they are part of something bigger than themselves? Explain.

5. Why are we so bent toward being "individuals"?

6. Why do you think Jesus chose to work in-depth with only twelve people?

IN OTHER WORDS . . .

I want to tell you a growing conviction with me, and that is that as we obey the leadings of the Spirit of God, we enable God to answer the prayers of other people. I mean that our lives, my life, is the answer to someone's prayer, prayed perhaps centuries ago.
—Oswald Chambers, dated February 16, 1907.

 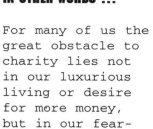

Take Home Page *continued*

DAILY READINGS AND REFLECTIONS

Devote yourself to the study of truth. Take a moment each day to read the following verses and then make journal notes related to the question for that day.

Monday—Read Ephesian 4:25. Paul encourages us to speak truth to our neighbor. What are the consequences of this in the body of Christ?

Tuesday—Read Psalm 15:1-3. David gives a few of the necessities for dwelling in the sanctuary of the Lord. Which one convicts you the most, and why?

Wednesday—Read Matthew 7:7-8. God tells His children that they can just ask if they have a need, and He will answer. Do you usually go to God first with all of your concerns?

Thursday—Read John 4:14. God promises to make us fountains of everlasting water. If He has done this in your life, are you keeping the floodgates open?

Friday—Read Ephesians 6:18. Our prayers must continue always unto heaven. In what ways could you characterize your life as a living prayer?

Saturday—Read Acts 2:42. Genuine devotion requires action. What are your acts of devotion these days?

TAKE INVENTORY

Answer these questions during the week to see how you are doing as a result of the lesson:

1. In what ways are you receiving truth each day?

2. How have you committed time and effort to your "team"?

3. Have you been involved in corporate prayer this week?

4. Have you given something away this week? What was it? How was it received?

THE NEXT STEP

1. Have a few new singles over for games and dessert. If possible, begin by playing a CD of "Old TV Theme Songs." Have everyone try to guess the titles to as many as they can.

2. Gather a few people to do some aerobics together once a week. Use a videotaped leader, so no one stresses out about leading the group.

3. Single Parent: During any time of the year, wrap a gift in Christmas paper and deliver to someone that your young child has really appreciated. Leave a note inside, from your child, that says "thank you" for all the things they do. Help your child deliver the present.

4. For a friend who isn't a Christian: Invite him or her over for dinner and a movie. But state in advance that you'd like to watch Franco Zeffirelli's "Jesus of Nazareth" together. Use the film as a starting point to ask what your friend thinks of Jesus. Naturally, you can take the opportunity to state your view of Jesus, too! (Idea: See if your friend would be willing to read one of the Gospel accounts of Jesus, in order to get the information straight from the best source.)

THINK—for Next Week: Do you have a team around you for support?

Session 3

The Strands of
SOLID UNITY

SESSION AIM

To help single adults recognize the attitudes and actions that contribute to strong bonds of group unity.

Ever taken flying lessons?

If so, you know that everything builds up to one big event: the day you'll be flying solo. No one else can do it for you. It's a one-person show.

Every day your singles are flying solo in a big and busy world. In so many ways, they've had to learn how to go it alone. That's why one of the huge jobs you face as a community builder is bringing the different personalities in your group together to function as a close-knit unit. It's tough, because our culture at large puts such emphasis on "looking out for number one."

The church, though, is different. Here in God's family we're to be interdependent, doing Kingdom work together as a vital, multi-faceted organism. The apostle Paul says it so well: "There is one body and one Spirit—just as you were called to one hope when you were called—one Lord, one faith, one baptism; one God and Father of all, who is over all and through all and in all" (Eph. 4:4-6).

This "one body" is what you want your singles to experience in your ministry. They need to know that God deeply desires harmony among them. Like the fragile, single strands of a rope, individuals can intertwine with the others. In this way, they'll form a strong and lasting cord, ready to do heavy work for God's glory.

WHAT'S IT ALL ABOUT?

Keep the following three Key Concepts in mind as you move through your session:

As individual strands in a rope, we must take on certain attitudes and actions to produce solid unity among us—

•Realize that humility is Job Number One.
•Revel in each other's differences.
•Run the second mile for one another.

BIBLE REFERENCES:

Ecclesiastes 4:12
Ephesians 4:2-3

Your 'Short Course' Set-Up...
(How to Use This Material in 35-45 Minutes)
Example: Sunday Morning Bible Study

1—Let's Get Started
(5-10 minutes)

Option 1: Them's Just Apples
Needed: One apple for each group, with an assortment of kinds and colors.

Tell small group members that they are the buyer for a local supermarket and that they must determine whether the store should buy these apples to sell in the future. Give each group an apple, and have the members judge it. Spend the first few minutes on the *looks* of the apple and then spend the remaining time on the *taste*.
Discuss:

•*How hard or difficult is it for you to be critical? Complimentary?*
•*When have you observed people being treated like these apples?*
•*What do we tend to do with "bad apples"—in our community? workplace? this group?*

Option 2: Picture Me Perfect
Needed: Several very small, empty picture frames.

Form groups of four to six people. Each person in the group will take the frame and hold it in front of a part of themselves that symbolizes a perceived weakness. He or she will then ask the group to guess what that weakness is. After everyone has had a turn, let volunteers share about how they have struggled with that area in their life and where they are in their attempts to deal with it. (Example: If John held the frame by his head, the group might guess his red hair. Then John might explain a childhood struggle with kids making fun of him. The group could affirm him and tell him he has the greatest hair ever.)
Discuss:

•*How could individual weaknesses contribute to a strong group unity?*

2—Looking to the Word
(15 minutes)

Present the mini-lecture found on pages 42-44. Have group members fill in the Key Concepts section on Interactive Page #1 as you speak.

3—Applying It to My Life
(5-10 minutes)

As soon as you complete your presentation, have small groups get together and go through the discussion questions in the "In My Opinion" section on Interactive Page #1.

4—Taking the Next Step
(5 minutes)

1. Direct attention to the "Summing the Scriptures" section of the Interactive Page #1. Ask individuals to work on their summaries in silence.
2. Then call the whole group together and invite volunteers to respond to the "ways I could contribute" question.

5—Let's Wrap It Up
(5 minutes)

1. Distribute the Take Home Page and make any necessary announcements.
2. If you have time, give people a chance to read and respond to "Time for a Response."
3. Spend some time in silent individual prayer for a stronger bond of unity in your group.

When You Have More Time...
(How to Use This Material in 60-90 Minutes)
Example: Small Groups at Home

1—Let's Get Started
(5-10 minutes)

Option 1: Take Out the Trash
Needed: Scrap newspaper or computer paper; masking tape; string; markers or crayons for each group.

Form teams and divide the room into squares (equal to the number of teams) using masking tape and string. Each square represents the team's "yard." Give each team member a piece of paper and a crayon in order to write (anonymously) a word describing something they don't like about other people. Then participants should crumple the paper into a ball.

When all the paper is crumpled, have everyone try to keep their "yard" clean by throwing all of their paper wads into someone else's yard. At the end of several half-minute rounds, count the paper in each team's yard and declare a total for the winning team. Finally, open up some of the paper wads and read the written words aloud. Discuss:

•*Have you ever been "treated like garbage"—because of your differences from others in a group?*

•*How do our dislikes affect our ability to work together in society? In groups like this?*

•*How do our differences prevent us from getting to know one another deeply?*

Option 2: Graffiti Poster
Needed: a large piece of poster board (or newsprint); tape; colored markers or crayons.

Tape the poster board on a wall and write at the top, in bold letters:

"True UNITY is..."

Then distribute colored markers or crayons. Ask your singles to think of what it means to work together as a close-knit unit in a singles group. Their task is to mark the poster with a piece of graffiti that indicates their idea. When everyone has had a chance to draw some graffiti, ask individuals to explain their entries.

2—Looking to the Word
(20-25 minutes)

Present the material found in "Presenting What the Bible Has to Say," on pages 42-44. Divide your allotted time into three segments: (1) Introduction, (2) Key Concepts, and (3) Conclusion. Keep your presentation short and to the point, drawing upon the "Going Deeper" information as appropriate.

3—Applying It to My Life
(20-25 minutes)

As soon as you complete your presentation, move to the "Challenging Characters Role Play," on Interactive Page #2.

4—Taking the Next Step
(10-20 minutes)

Now go to the "Focus on the Single" discussion activity on Interactive Page #2. Do the activity in small groups. Give each group a different topic and have its members discuss the topic using all of their professional knowledge. Have small groups report a summary of each broadcast to the large group.

5—Let's Wrap It Up
(5 minutes)

1. Make your group's announcements at this time.
2. Distribute the Take Home Page and give everyone a chance to consider "Time for a Response."

HINT:

Remember to plan plenty of interaction time in your small group settings. Watch for potential leaders and begin early to use their gifts and encourage the development of their potential.

Extending The Learning...
(How to Use This Material in Two Hours)
Example: Extended Week-Night Program

1—Let's Get Started
(20-30 minutes)

Option 1: Traffic Jam
Needed: a 2x6 board, about 16 or 20 feet long.

Lay the board on the floor or ground and form teams. Have each team split in two and stand on opposite ends of the board facing each other. The two groups are to switch ends of the board without touching the ground. If anyone falls off, have them go back one transfer-place to where they started before they stepped off. Begin like this: > > > > > < < < < < End like this: < < < < < > > > > >
Discuss:

•How well did you work together as a team?
•When you deal with people, do you tend to kneel down and serve, or are you looking for ways to step over others?
•Did any person clearly demonstrate humility in this activity? In what ways?

Option 2: Direct Me
Needed: Construction paper; crayons or markers.

Ask pairs of people to sit back-to-back. Have each partner draw a picture of his or her childhood bedroom, with as much detail as possible. Then have each person, one at a time, *describe* their picture to their partner, in order for them to draw it. Focus on listening skills and taking interest in the other person. Then bring the whole group together and discuss:

•Who was able to most closely duplicate a bedroom from verbal instructions?
•Are you surprised at how different the pictures look?
• To what extent do we judge others by what we hear—and then get the totally wrong picture? Can you give an example from your own experience or observation?

2—Looking to the Word
(20-25 minutes)

Present the material found in "Presenting What the Bible Has to Say," on pages 42-44. Parcel your time between the three segments: (1) Introduction, (2) Key Concepts, (3) Conclusion.

3—Applying It to My Life
(30-40 minutes)

As soon as you complete your presentation, form small groups. Have each small group list—within seven minutes—as many things as possible that its members have in common. Then compare all of the groups together to see what they had in common. (You may also wish to do a "spiritual inventory" in these small groups to find out how God has done similar things in each person's life.)

•When you first meet someone, do you tend to seek out commonalities or differences to talk about?
•Why might we tend to focus on people's differences rather than on things we have in common?
•How can we create an environment of acceptance in a singles group?

4—Taking the Next Step
(30-40 minutes)

First, spend some time in silent prayer. Then come together in groups of three to pray for each other. Generate prayer concerns by focusing on how group members would like to "go the extra mile" for one another during the week ahead.

5—Let's Wrap It Up
(5 minutes)

1. Make your group's announcements at this time.
2. If time permits, and it seems appropriate for your group, wrap up by using the activity option "Humble Feat" on page 46.
3. Distribute the Take Home Page and close in prayer.

My Personal Game Plan

STEP 1   Time: _____ minutes.

Materials Needed:

Activities Summary:

STEP 2   Time: _____ minutes.

Materials Needed:

Activities Summary:

STEP 3   Time: _____ minutes.

Materials Needed:

Activities Summary:

STEP 4   Time: _____ minutes.

Materials Needed:

Activities Summary:

STEP 5   Time: _____ minutes.

Materials Needed:

Activities Summary:

Just for You
Teacher's Devotional

Writer John Selden said, "Humility is a virtue all preach, none practice, and everybody is content to hear."

As leaders, sometimes we mistakenly believe that we have to come across as bold and strong in order for people to listen to us. Yet, when we consider the many words of Christ to His disciples, we are caressed by His humble tones. Recall how He handled the sometimes utter stupidity of a group of twelve men who... just didn't get it.

Of course, it would have been easy for Jesus to confront their lack of faith by performing awesome supernatural acts. Instead, He most often gently guided them through the questions of life. And He did it with a graciousness and compassion that was grounded in humility.

Suppose our singles saw us as the disciples saw Jesus? As a humble servant willing to draw attention only to God?

Humility is a quiet thing, yet it can speak so loudly of God's sufficiency in our lives. Concentrate this week on being intentionally humble in your world, as you meditate upon such verses as Micah 6:8 and Isaiah 30:15. Be content to speak kind, gentle, and compassionate words to the singles that God has entrusted to your care.

—Joel and Kent

- TO HELP SINGLE ADULTS
  _____
  _____
  _____

- TO HELP SINGLE ADULTS
  _____
  _____
  _____

- TO HELP SINGLE ADULTS
  _____
  _____
  _____

- TO HELP SINGLE ADULTS
  _____
  _____
  _____

WHAT I LEARNED FROM READING 'LOOKING TO THE WORD' . . .

Notes and Insights—

Presenting What the Bible Has to Say...

Use the mini-lecture below to cover this session's biblical Key Concepts. Study the outline carefully, adding your own personal illustrations to make it your own. Special instructions to you are in bold type.

Introduction

Start with an object lesson. Bring in a nine-foot piece of rope and demonstrate some of its various uses: tieing some cool knots, jumping rope, tieing a rolled-up sleeping bag, etc. After your little demonstration, have two people hold both ends of the rope. Cut or chop the rope in half in front of the group. Show the group that many individual strands actually make up a rope. Pull on some of the strands so they can see this visual picture. (NOTE: If you can cut up an old climbing rope, the illustration would be more powerful; a climbing rope has countless tiny strands.)

THE KEY CONCEPTS

Transition statement: The Bible says in Ecclesiastes 4:12, "Though one may be overpowered, two can defend themselves. A cord of three strands is not quickly broken." This verse tells us about the power of a unit over the strength of an individual. The world we live in champions the individual "strand" philosophy. But we—our church, our team—champion the cause of "stranding together" as a unit. Like the rope before it is cut, we want to be a strong unit, tied together, able to accomplish multiple tasks.

Today we're going to talk about the role that each one of us plays in the stranding together of our group. As individual strands in a rope, we must take on certain attitudes and actions to produce solid unity among us—

KEY CONCEPT #1:
Realize that humility is Job Number One.

Read Ephesians 4:2-3 aloud.

Illustration. **Tell everyone about the first job you had as a young person. Go into some detail concerning what you liked and disliked about that job. If there is time, ask a few volunteers to quickly describe their first jobs, too.**

My first job was an important part of my maturing as a man/woman. The first job that we have with each other in community is the practice of humility. Yes—sometimes it is a tough job. It requires effort, focus, and quite a bit of hard work. But it is such an important part of "us" maturing together as close-knit group.

Briefly discuss:

•*What do you think it means to be completely humble?*
•*Who have you known to display this quality in an excellent way?*

Humility is the ability to have an objective view of ourselves, without pride, and without false self-effacement. How do we acquire it? Consider:

Now offer these subpoints—

(1) Humility requires vulnerability. One of the most important things we can offer to each other is our weaknesses and vulnerability. When we're willing to share these things, we give others a chance to be heroes in our lives. If we can never be needy, we are actually being selfish—refusing to give others the chance to be helpers.

(2) Humility shines through in a learner's spirit. A learner's spirit releases God's power to work within our group for unity. It is a willingness on everyone's part to approach the table of life with a desire to take in new things offered by others. It is the exact opposite of a "BTDT attitude" (been there; done that).

(3) Humility is expressed by a grateful heart. A grateful person is constantly offering thanksgiving for the person God is making her, and for the people that God has placed in her life. Unfortunately, this is not our natural tendency. As Mark Twain once said: "If you pick up a starving dog and make him prosperous, he will not bite you. This is the principal difference between a dog and a man." No biting in this group!

KEY CONCEPT #2:
Revel in each other's differences.

Illustration. **Bring five balls to the meeting. Make sure that three of the balls are exactly alike (tennis balls would work), the two remaining balls need to be different (a basketball, a Nerf ball, golf ball). Ask the group which of the balls doesn't belong in the group. The answer is obvious. (By the way, if you remember the old *Sesame Street* song, "one of these things just doesn't belong here," you could sing it for the group. They would die laughing at you, but that's a good thing.)**

This is what some Christians can tend to do with each other. It's called "selection," based on how you look, what you do, what you like, etc. If I don't think you belong, I will act that way toward you. As a matter of fact, I will tell others about you being a "different" ball, and hope that they will think that you don't belong as well.

Read Ephesians 4:2 (with focus on the end of verse 2: "bearing with one another in love").
Ask:

•*Have you ever had to "bear with someone in love"? What did that mean for you? How easy or difficult is it?*
•*When has someone had to do the same toward you?*

Let me suggest that "bearing with one another in love" involves reveling in each other's differences. It is accepting each other with a "clean slate," accepting despite our many flaws and foibles.

To *revel* means "to make merry." We need to celebrate our differences. In order to have an awesome party, you need an awe-some party host. That is what each of us needs to be—a party host. We invite people into our lives and celebrate who they are—the person that God made them to be. So let's remember that we are all different in a good way. Like a quilt with many different colors and patterns, we can be woven together by our God for His glory. **(If you can bring in a quilt to illustrate this point, it would be all the more powerful).**

KEY CONCEPT #3:
Run the second mile for one another.

Illustration. **Begin your third point by offering the "Second Mile Club" illustration.**

We need to go the second mile for one another if we are to develop strong unity. Consider just four people who joined the Second Mile Club:

Michaelangelo's painting "The Last Judgment" was one of the twelve master paintings of the ages. It took eight years of hard work. *George Stephenson* spent 15 years perfecting the locomotive engine. *Goodyear* worked for ten years in poverty and public ridicule before perfecting hard rubber. *Westinghouse* was treated as a lunatic by most railroad executives. Yet, he held up under the pressure and finally sold his air-brake system.

•*Can you think of other two-milers? Famous people? Folks in your own world? You?*

Read Ephesians 4:3 (Focus on the beginning of verse 3: "make every effort.")

Subpoints to emphasize—
(1) The second mile is a great relational gift. If our goal is to become a tight unit, one of the greatest things we can give to each other is a "second-mile rule" in our relationships. It's a willingness to do as this verse says, "make every effort to keep the unity." This will require our sweat as well. It will mean that we offer each other grace in the midst of adversity.

(2) Running the second mile helps resolve conflicts. "Making every effort" also requires a willingness to resolve

HINT:

Teach with an open Bible, rather than reading Scriptures from a study guide or some other source. Also, be sensitive to those who many be uncomfortable reading or praying aloud. Never take turns reading or praying around the the room; don't just call on someone to pray unless you know their comfort level.

conflicts in a healthy manner. Many Christians rip each other apart because they refuse to handle conflict in a Christlike manner. Instead, they become embittered and angry. The first step is to approach the other person to say: "I want our friendship to grow. How can we solve this together?" Then you put the problem on the table in front of you and attack it with your combined resources. That's unity.

Conclusion

Becoming a unit is tough work. No doubt even Jesus had a difficult time unifying His band of desert followers. They were all sinners, like you and me. They struggled with pride, and with not accepting each other. Yet Christ did a great work in their lives.

Christ wants to do a great work in our lives, too. He understands us; He knows our weaknesses. Yet He wants us to lay down our pride differences, and expectations. He desires unity among us, for He prayed in John 17:11: "Father, protect them by the power of your name...so that they may be one as we are one."

And Christ implores us through His Word to make every effort to keep the unity. It is His invitation to "let it all out" with each other—to be real, to be humble, to throw a party for each other on a daily basis, and to join the Second Mile Club when it comes to our issues with each other. What about you? Which one of these points did you need to hear about today? Let's pray for us; let's pray about our own unity.

GOING DEEPER

Mini-background on Ephesians. The church at Ephesus was established in A.D. 53. Paul had spent over three years with the Ephesian church. As a result, he was very close to these believers.

This letter was not written to counteract heresy,

as with some of the other churches that Paul helped plant. Rather, it was a letter of encouragement that probably circulated among many churches in the region. In it Paul describes the nature and appearance of the church, and he challenges believers to function as the living body of Christ on earth. He also explains the wonderful blessings—or "riches"—that we have received through Christ, referring to the church as a body, a temple, a bride, and a soldier. These all illustrate *a unity of purpose* and show how each individual member is a part that must work together with all the other parts.

A key statement related to this session comes in Ephesians 4:4-6— "There is one body and one Spirit—just as you were called to one hope when you were called—one Lord, one faith, one baptism; one God and Father of all, who is over all and through all and in all."

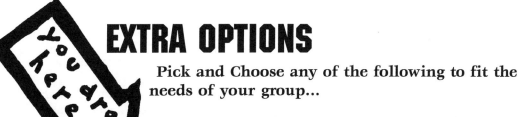

EXTRA OPTIONS

Pick and Choose any of the following to fit the needs of your group...

Options to Consider...for Step 1

Spider Web

Needed: 30 feet of string and two upright poles (volleyball standards) or anchor points to tie string into. Construct a "spider web" by tieing a string to four points on each of the poles. The idea is to make various sizes of holes to allow for different-sized people.

Tell teams of six to ten people that they are to put everyone through a different hole in the web without touching the string. If they touch, they must start that person over again. They may begin with people on both sides of the web for safety, but a major rule is that the individual lays very rigid with no movement. No jumping through the holes—everyone must be passed through. (If someone is really struggling, adjust the string for the group in order to accommodate.) The idea is for everyone to understand: They are part of a team and each person is to be loved in their differences. Discuss:

•When have you failed to "pass through" a group's web of acceptance? What was apparently required of you? How did you feel?

•What do we require of people around here—in order to "pass"?

All Aboard!

Needed: One three-foot-square cardboard platform for each group.

Form groups of people, in numbers that would barely be able to fit on the cardboard platforms. Describe the task of getting everyone on their "cardboard island," because there are man-eating alligators coming to feast. Everyone in the group must get onto the platform and hold their position while singing "Jesus Loves Me." Participants may not touch the floor, but they must alert the group if they are falling so others can let go of them in order to prevent the whole group from falling over. Also, keep everyone's feet below the waist (no one on shoulders).

After the activity, discuss:

•What was it like being so close to one another?

•Did anyone have time to notice each other's differences? Were you able to get along inside of those differences?

•Where does one go for acceptance and closeness as a single in the world? How could we do better at keeping our singles on the platform of Christian community?

Options to Consider...for Step 3

Mirror Image—Get into a large circle where everyone can see each other clearly. Instruct everyone to begin acting out their favorite sport or hobby. Then have the group look at one person and do exactly what that person is doing. How quickly can the whole group change to doing just one thing? Do this a few times, then follow up with discussion about the challenge of individuals being called to work as a unified group in God's kingdom.

45

Bumper Stickers—Tell the group that they are helping to make slogans for the church "Bumper Sticker Program" and that they need to develop slogans related to the Key Concepts of this lesson. Have a competition to see who can generate the most and the best slogans. Let the group judge themselves.

Options to Consider...for Step 4

Stand-up Helpers—To get a better focus on humility and gentleness, have each person in the group sit down on the floor. Then, without using their hands and keeping their feet flat on the floor, have everyone try to stand up. They will find it very difficult. Then have them grab a partner to sit behind them. Using each other without locking arms, try to stand up. Make the point: If everyone depends on one another and supports one another, our lives in Christ can be filled with joy and effectiveness.

The Great Egg Drop

Needed: For each group you will need: one raw egg (and a couple more for accidents); ten inches of masking tape; ten plastic drinking straws; a plastic garbage bag; a step ladder.

Form groups of 3-6 people to design a "crash cage" for an egg that will be dropped from a height of eight feet. In a successful drop, the egg's shell will remain intact.

Say: "You have been commissioned by NASA to design the first egg-manned space capsule to Mars. Your mission, if you choose to accept it, will be to use the masking tape and straws to build a structure around the egg, preventing the egg from breaking on impact with the ground."

Spread the garbage bag out below the drop site and give the groups about ten minutes to plan and build their cages. Then everyone goes to the ladder to take a turn at dropping. Later, throw out the question:

•*Are we gentle enough with people as to not break their shells? What does this kind of gentleness look like in real-life situations?*

Options to Consider...for Step 5

Plank Eye—End the evening by taking a lighthearted look at yourself and some of your differences—things that might affect people around you. Have everyone go to various people in the room and say, "I'm sorry I'm so…" People will be surprised at the responses they receive. Discuss those responses.

Humble Feat—Bring out a small wash basin filled with warm water. Make wash cloths and foot powder available. Then have each person choose someone whose feet they will wash. (Have them ask kindly.) Impress upon the group that allowing oneself to be served is equal to the act of service. This may be a struggle for some because they are usually the ones doing all the "washing" in a group!
Discussion:

•*How did you feel as you were washing, or being washed?*
•*Were either of you concerned about what others might think?*
•*Why put powder on the feet? What was this a sign of?*
•*How could this activity affect your everyday life?*

Interactive Page 1

IN MY OPINION . . .

•What part does humility and gentleness play in our relationships with each other? Can you give a practical example?

•When have you been quite open and vulnerable with someone? Did this turn out to be a positive experience, or not?

•In your life, do you tend to celebrate other's differences? Or do those differences tend to hinder your relationship?

•What is your typical inner reaction when you are asked to "go the extra mile" for someone? (Choose one, and explain.)

___ Who, *me?* (I'm afraid I lack the qualifications.)

___ You're kidding, right? (Like I have nothing else to do.)

___ I'd be happy to help. (I'd be happy to help.)

___ I'd be happy to help. (No, I would *not* be happy to help.)

___ Only one mile? Why not four or five? Why not a long, cross-country trek? (Hey, they don't call me Mr. Doormat for nothing!)

KEY CONCEPTS
on Solid Unity

As individual "strands" in a rope, we must take three key actions for God to bring us together in a solid unity—

#1 Realize that _____ is _____.

#2 _____ in each other's _____.

#3 Run the_____ _____for one another.

SUMMING THE SCRIPTURES

Look up a Scripture passage below and write a short summary of what the passage means to you, personally. Be ready to report: *How could I encourage the other group members about my role here—about ways I think I can contribute?*

•2 Corinthians 5:11-21
•1 Corinthians 4:1-5
•Romans 14:1-15:7
•James 2:1-13
•James 4:11-12
•Matthew 7:1-5
•Matthew 5:43-48

Summary of_____:

Though one may be overpowered, two can defend themselves. A cord of three strands is not quickly broken.
—Ecclesiastes 4:12

Be completely humble and gentle; be patient, bearing with one another in love. 3 Make every effort to keep the unity of the Spirit through the bond of peace.
—Ephesians 4:2-3

47

Though one may be overpowered, two can defend themselves. A cord of three strands is not quickly broken.
—Ecclesiastes 4:12

Be completely humble and gentle; be patient, bearing with one another in love. 3 Make every effort to keep the unity of the Spirit through the bond of peace.
—Ephesians 4:2-3

'CHALLENGING CHARACTER'S ROLEPLAY

Form small groups. Each person choose to be one of the characters below. In character, take turns completing this statement:

The way people usually show their dislike for me is by . . . .

I'm in a wheelchair
I don't make much money
I'm a joker
I'm overweight
I'm homosexual
I'm white (or: I'm Black, Hispanc, Asian, etc.)
I'm shy
I'm extroverted
I don't speak the language very well
I'm addicted
I have an illness
Other: _____

Now go back to being yourself, and discuss:

•*How does it feel to be "different" in a roleplay? In real life?*
•*What things could a person do in order to become more tolerant of differences?*
•*What moral absolutes might prevent the tolerance of certain behaviors? Would this limit our love for people, as well? Explain.*

KEY CONCEPTS
on Solid Unity

As individual "strands" in a rope, we must take three key actions for God to bring us together in a solid unity—

#1 Realize that _____is _____.

#2 _____in each other's_____.

#3 Run the _____ _____ for one another.

FOCUS ON THE SINGLE

Imagine your group serves as a "panel of experts" during a famous radio broadcast called "Focus on the Single." Choose a topic:

•Being a friend to a person of the opposite sex, without turning them on
•Finding humility in everyday life
•The greatest act of service a single can do
•Dating the non-Christian
•Stories of gentleness
•How do we become so closed minded?
•Why is it so hard to love in spite of differences?

Take Home Page

ABC

TIME FOR A RESPONSE

The most personally relevant thing I've learned in this session is:

[ ]

How can I apply the three Key Concepts?

In my time with God:

In my personal life:

In my church/personal ministry:

In my community:

In my workplace:

In my friendships:

As a single parent (teaching this principle to my kids):

With my roommate(s):

FINISH THE THOUGHT

1. My ability to not be selfish lies in how I...

_____

_____

_____.

2. The moment I think about walking a second mile with someone I...

_____

_____

_____.

Take Home Page ABC continued

DAILY READINGS AND REFLECTIONS

In your devotions this week, consider some of the imperfect people Jesus loved and befriended. Write some journal entries related to these stories and the questions that follow.

Monday—"Woman at the Well" (John 4:1-26)
Tuesday—"Man with Leprosy" (Matt. 8:1-4)
Wednesday—"Zacheus the Tax Collector" (Luke 19:1-10)
Thursday—"Woman caught in Adultery" (John 8:1-11)
Friday—"Demon-possessed Daughter" (Matt. 15:21-28)
Saturday—"Sinful Woman" (Luke 7:36-50)

How did Jesus approach this sinner? What incredible thing did Jesus do in this life? How would I have reacted if I were the one confronted by Jesus? If I were Jesus? In my daily life, do I tend to focus more on *the behavior* or on *the person?*

THE NEXT STEP

(Projects and Ideas for the Week Ahead)

•Bring a few people together for a "Scum Party" at your church. Look around and make a list of all the jobs that are really gross but need doing. Clean out the boiler room and the bathrooms? Spruce up the nursery, the windows, the kitchen floors, the lights? Or paint the trim around the building?

•Cook extra food for Sunday's lunch and go to church, making it your goal to invite someone home for lunch. Make it someone you may not know or want to know better. Take a risk, and pray about it beforehand. Plan to focus on your guest and what is happening in his or her life. For example: have them bring over a recent video of their vacation, or of childhood pictures. Take pains to be involved in this person!

•Throw a party for someone in your life that really needs encouragement. Whoop it up! Invite all his or her friends over and have them plan to bring pictures or tell some of the great stories from the past.

FINISH THE THOUGHT...

• The greatest good one person can do for another is to...

RANDOM ACTS OF KINDNESS

Go for It! Take some of these ideas and run with them. Spur of the moment is best.

Roommates: Movie Time—Rent the old classics and do some nachos and queso!

Single Parents: Rent "Rigelleto" and talk about the movie afterwards.

Older Singles: Do some antique shopping together for someone specific. Try to find objects they may have a special interest in. Thimbles, watches, silverware, tools, or jewelry?

THINK—for Next Week: What is your ultimate ambition in life?

IN OTHER WORDS...

There is a kind of happiness and wonder that makes you serious.
—C.S. Lewis, *The Last Battle*

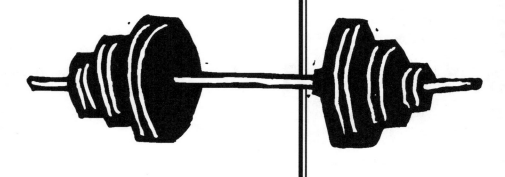

Session 4
AN ETERNAL
Ambition

Someone has said, "Many a man with an ambition to find fame and fortune failed because he didn't find himself first." No doubt the better statement would be, "...he or she failed because of not finding CHRIST first."

It's easy for any of us to get caught up in the bump and grind of striving for success. After all, everywhere we turn we're reminded of the apparent importance of personal performance. Star athletes look into the TV camera and proclaim: "You can do anything if you want it bad enough." And then there's the commercial that says, "A man *is* what a man *does.*"

Personal ambition has its place, of course. But have we forgotten the legitimate role of *spiritual ambition?* The Bible puts it this way: "Do you not know that in a race all the runners run, but only one gets the prize? Run in such a way as to get the prize" (1 Cor. 9:24). The best prize of all is to take on the character of Jesus.

This is a back-to-the-basics session about spiritual ambition. It suggests that as we all hold to the same goal—growth in Christ—we actually strengthen the bonds of community in His Kingdom. United in this eternal purpose, we unite in earthly fellowship. Therefore, invite your singles to come to this firm conclusion for themselves: that finding and pursuing Christ is by far the greatest pursuit of life itself. And it's also the best way to help their group grow strong in the bonds of mutual love.

SESSION AIM

To help singles recognize that the greatest ambition of their lives should be the pursuit of Christ—internally, personally, and externally. When all are involved in this pursuit, community happens.

WHAT'S IT ALL ABOUT?

These Key Concepts ought to come through as you move through your session:

Though salvation comes only by the grace of God, growing in Christ is the greatest ambition we can have. So let's…

• Work at changing for Christ—internally.
• Work at growing and maturing in Christ—personally.
• Work at giving Christ to each other—externally.

BIBLE REFERENCES:

Philippians 3:7-8
1 Corinthians 3:11-15

Your 'Short Course' Set-Up...
(How to Use This Material in 35-45 Minutes)
Example: Sunday Morning Bible Study

1—Let's Get Started
(5-10 minutes)

Option 1: Inflated Success
Needed: One balloon per person.

Ask everyone to gather into small groups and distribute balloons. Group members should blow up their balloons as big as they can and then tie them. Distribute markers and have participants write entries on their balloons in response to this instruction: Name all of the things you believe demonstrate success in the world, as you think in terms of corporate America.

Then give the small groups a chance to discuss:

•*To what extent is the common view of success "inflated" (i.e., too "high priced," or likely to "explode" on a person)?*
•*What is your own, personal definition of a successful life?*

Option 2: Fire In the Hole!
Start with the opener activity on Interactive Page #1 titled "Fire in the Hole." After spending some time on the two discussion questions, move to your Bible presentation.

Option 3: Discussion Time
Use the "Whaddaya Think?" discussion questions on Interactive Page #1. You may wish to have partners or small buzz groups consider the questions. Assign all or some of the questions to each group, then have groups report their insights.

Note: If time or interest allows, use additional options found on pages 59-60.

2—Looking to the Word
(10-20 minutes)

Offer the "Presenting What the Bible Has to Say," material found on pages 56-58. Organize your presentation under the three segments: Introduction, Key Concepts, and Conclusion. Keep your energy level high as you speak, drawing upon the "Going Deeper" information whenever as appropriate.

3—Applying It to My Life
(5-10 minutes)

After your presentation, direct attention to the "Ambition Self-Evaluator" section on the Take Home Page. Allow individuals time to evaluate themselves in silence, using this tool. Then ask volunteers to share their insights. Follow up with this general discussion question:

•*In your opinion, what is God's view of our career ambitions?*

4—Taking the Next Step
(10 minutes)

You may now use the "Incomplete Completions" exercise on Interactive Page #1. Your singles may work alone or in pairs, but emphasize that they will only need to reveal what they feel comfortable sharing. Partners may ask one another for prayer related to the sentences.

5—Let's Wrap It Up
(5 minutes)

Make any necessary announcements for the coming week at this time, and dismiss the group with your favorite benediction.

HINT:

These opener activities are great for quickly getting people loosened up and interacting. Draw out spiritual applications, or simply use them as icebreakers. But don't spend a lot of time explaining; keep your directions short and simple.

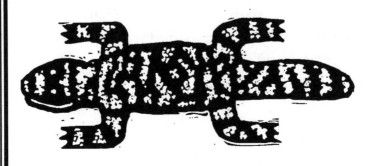

1—Let's Get Started
(5-10 minutes)

Option 1: Everybody Up!

Have the whole group form a circle, with everyone holding hands. Explain that everyone is going to form a shape by moving as a group. The catch is that group members will keep their eyes closed.

Begin by calling out a shape and then have the group try to make it. Use a time limit to determine when participants can open their eyes and view the result. Some of the shapes you can suggest: Square, Triangle, Rectangle, Star, Cross, Shamrock (for the bigger groups). After a few rounds, discuss:

•*In what ways have you noticed us moving and adjusting as a group to the will of God during the past year?*
•*How could we do better at this?*

Option 2: Silly Debate

Needed: A bag of Oreo™ cookies; two podiums or small lecterns.

Ask the two funniest people in the group to go to the front of the room—to lecterns, if possible—for a silly debate. Inform the group that you will now hold a debate on the Oreo™ Cookie! (Hold up a cookie and ask everyone to concentrate on it for a moment.) Then proceed with this theme:

Resolved: The cream filling inside is better than the chocolaty cookie outside.

One person will argue for the cream and the other for the cookie. Split the group and have one half cheer for the cream and the other half for the cookie. End the debate by saying, "Time is up. Thank you both for the insightful debate . . . *but who really cares?*" Then offer everyone an Oreo™ before your Bible presentation.

Use the debate as an illustration of how everyone in the group was *focused on the same thing* at the beginning, but how easy it was to get sidetracked.

Option 3: Interact / Discussion

Begin your session with the activity on Interactive Page #2, titled "Ambitious...Or Not?"

Note: If time or interest allows, use additional options found on pages 59-60.

2—Looking to the Word
(20-30 minutes)

Present the "What the Bible Has to Say," material found on pages 56-58. Use the "Going Deeper" information whenever you think it would be appropriate.

3—Applying It to My Life
(20-25 minutes)

Needed: 3x5 notecards and pencils.

As soon as you complete your presentation, distribute a notecard and a pencil to every member. Give these instructions: "Summarize the presentation you've just heard in two to seven words, using language that a three-year-old could quickly grasp." Have everyone write their summaries on the cards before sharing them aloud. Vote on the clearest summary, then spend some time brainstorming:

•*What are your practical ideas on how to apply all of this theology in daily life?*

4—Taking the Next Step
(10-20 minutes)

Needed: Half sheets of poster board for individuals or partners, colored markers.

Do the "Vulnerability Inventory" activity on Interactive page #2.

5—Let's Wrap It Up
(5 minutes)

1. In small groups, have each group designate someone to read Philippians 1:20-21 aloud. Offer prayers focused on applying these verses in one anothers' lives.

2. Now make your group's announcements and distribute the Take Home Page.

Extending The Learning...
(How to Use This Material in Two Hours)
Example: Extended Week-Night Program

1—Let's Get Started
(20-30 minutes)

Option 1: Stepping Stones Initiative

Needed: Six 2"x4"x8" pieces of wood for each group. You may obtain scrap boards and cut them down to size. Alternatives: Use pieces of paper, bricks, or something that two people can step on without touching the floor.

Have everyone put on blindfolds, except for one person. The object of this initiative is for the group to get across a lava pit, roughly 20 feet long, with only the use of the stepping stones (blocks of wood). The limitation is that the stones must always remain in contact with the people. This means they cannot simply throw the blocks of wood down and then jump on them. They must maintain contact with blocks at all times, hands or feet. You may choose to inflict a punishment on a group that forgets this rule by taking a block away for every infraction. After the activity, discuss:

•*How was the concentration required for this activity like, and unlike, trying to keep our focus on Christ daily?*

Option 2: Strung Along

Needed: A long rope or string; blindfolds.

Choose a safe path for everyone to walk through the building, yard, or nearby woods. Prepare for safety by clearing anything that will poke or trip. You may want to place a spotter near questionable areas to help everyone. Take your rope along the path, tieing it so that it hangs right at the waist. Then have everyone get into a single-file line on the rope, blindfolded. The object will be for the group to walk along the rope, silently, totally trusting the rope to guide them. At the end of the course, discuss:

•*When have you had to put total trust in God? In another person?*
•*How hard or easy is it for you to let go of personal ambition and expertise in order to trust another's skills?*

Option 3: Discussion Questions

Use the "Ambition Self-Evaluator" activity on the Take Home Page to begin your session. Ask volunteers to comment on their responses before moving to Step 2.

2—Looking to the Word
(20-30 minutes)

Gather everyone for "Presenting What the Bible Has to Say," found on pages 565-8. Prepare this mini-talk ahead of time, blending in your own life experiences and personal illustrations. Make this presentation your own!

3—Applying It to My Life
(30-40 minutes)

As soon as you complete your presentation, direct everyone's attention to the "In Other Words" section on the Take Home Page. Count off by fours and assign a quotation to each individua.l. Answer the three questions under "Quote Reactions."

4—Taking the Next Step
(15-20 minutes)

Tell everyone that they will have the opportunity to spend ten minutes alone in "prayer listening" regarding their relationship with Christ. Ask them to approach God with these words, and then to spend time simply *listening* for the Lord in silence:

Lord, I want to focus my ambition on spiritual growth. What is the next step to take?

5—Let's Wrap It Up
(5 minutes)

Needed: A potted plant.

Close with a brief object lesson. Use a potted plant to explain: this plant's only desire in life *is to grow.* This should be our primary desire, as well—to know Christ and His fullness and to have a deeper relationship with God our Father. But we allow self-interest to kill us, just like the roots of a plant not getting proper nutrients, water, or sun. Feed yourself with the Word this week! As we all do so, we will grow strong *together* in Christ!

My Personal Game Plan

STEP 1   Time: _____ minutes.

Materials Needed:

Activities Summary:

STEP 2   Time: _____ minutes.

Materials Needed:

Activities Summary:

STEP 3   Time: _____ minutes.

Materials Needed:

Activities Summary:

STEP 4   Time: _____ minutes.

Materials Needed:

Activities Summary:

STEP 5   Time: _____ minutes.

Materials Needed:

Activities Summary:

Just for You
Teacher's Devotional

What's it like in your inner world? Jesus was extremely concerned about this. In Matthew 23:25, He said to the Pharisees, "Woe to you, teachers of the law and Pharisees, you hypocrites! You clean the outside of the cup and dish, but inside they are full of greed and self indulgence."

We hear a lot today about "fallen teachers"—people who have taken the big trip down the mountainside because of some grievous sin that entangled their footsteps. What is it in your inner world right now that could trip you up? What could keep your teaching from being the most powerful it could possibly be?

It's easy for our singles to view us as leaders that "have it all together." But what they don't know is . . . we really don't! One of the most significant things you can do for your singles group is to clean the *inside* of your cup and dish, and keep it clean every day. This will allow you to be used to your max for the Master. So take some time to consider—

•The area of my life where temptation hits the hardest is:

•How I *usually* handle my temptations:

•How I'd *like* to handle the next temptation coming my way:

Christ loves using clean, healthy vessels. What will you need to do in order to "wash up"?

—Joel and Kent

MY GOALS FOR THIS SESSION:

- **TO HELP SINGLE ADULTS**
  _____
  _____
  _____

- **TO HELP SINGLE ADULTS**
  _____
  _____
  _____

- **TO HELP SINGLE ADULTS**
  _____
  _____
  _____

- **TO HELP SINGLE ADULTS**
  _____
  _____
  _____

WHAT I LEARNED FROM READING 'LOOKING TO THE WORD' . . .

Notes and Insights—

LOOKING TO THE WORD—AN ETERNAL AMBITION

Presenting
What the Bible Has to Say...

Here's your mini-lecture covering the biblical Key Concepts. Try to become familiar with the flow of thoughts, and the outline, in order to present this material with maximum eye contact. Special instructions to you are in bold type. (Note: Have group members refer to the Key Concepts section on their Interactive Page. They may wish to fill in the blanks as you speak.)

Introduction

Tell this story as your opening illustration:

A famous pastor from the Midwest was sailing with his wife in the Caribbean. One night they pulled into a harbor, where he docked beside a group of people who were "partying down" on another boat. The party group asked the pastor and his wife if they wanted to join them for dinner. The pastor kindly consented, thinking that this would be a great evangelism opportunity.

During dinner, the conversation turned to what the pastor did for a living, and the partyers were somewhat embarrassed when they found that they were getting drunk in the presence of a minister. After dinner, the pastor and his wife excused themselves, and as they were disembarking from the boat, one of the partyers boldly called out, "By the way, what does it mean to have a personal relationship with Jesus?"

The pastor knew he only had about 30 seconds of attention span to convey the gospel message. He said, "When you think of religion, you think of two letters—D, O. When you think of Christ, and having a personal relationship with Him, you think of four letters—D, O, N, E! Knowing Christ means responding to what He has already DONE for you and I on the cross."

Transition statement: Today we want to talk about Jesus Christ. We could attempt to put into practice a variety of methods in order to become a loving and healthy community. But nothing is more crucial to community than our own personal relationships with Jesus. The difference between having a religion, and having a relationship with Christ is monumental. He desires for each of us to respond with gratitude every day to what He has done for us—to fall fervently in love with Him and to know Him better every day. This is the kind of stuff that genuine community is built upon. When we as individuals are deeply in love with Christ, that love has the power to permeate our community and draw us together in an eternal bond.

Though salvation comes only by the grace of God, growing in Christ is the greatest ambition we can have. So let's—

- Work at changing for Christ—internally.
- Work at growing and maturing in Christ—personally.
- Work at giving Christ to each other—externally.

THE KEY CONCEPTS

Read Philippians 3:7-8 aloud. Clue your group into the fact that this was Paul's own "personal mission statement."

KEY CONCEPT #1:
We must WORK at changing for Christ—internally.

Illustration. **"My Private World." Bring in some of the things in your life that you consider private—things such as: your wallet, your checkbook, your journal. Or, talk about some of the other things that are private in your life: your glove box, boxes in your basement or attic, your photo albums, etc. Say:**

Without a doubt we all have things and parts of our lives that we consider quite private. I mean think about it—we don't go rummaging around in each other's glove compartment, wallet, or checkbook whenever we desire. The same holds true with your relationship with Christ. There is a private "inner world" that Christ lives in as well. It's the part that the majority of people don't know about. Unfortunately, it can sometimes be the smelly part.

Now make these points:

(1) Someone has said, "Who you are in your private world is *who you really are* in your public world."

•*How do you respond to that statement?*

(2) If we really expect and want to grow in Christ, we must be willing to deal with the private sins, private past, and private problem-issues of our lives.

(3) Your inner/private world is where Jesus wants to be Master.

•*What are some of the moves that we need to make in order to see that happen?*

(4) One of the greatest gifts you can give to this team is your real inside self. Once that begins to happen with a few people, others begin to see that they can be free to do the same thing. You are immediately placing value on being real for Christ. As we build trust in one another this way, we build community.

KEY CONCEPT #2:
We must work at growing and maturing in Christ— personally

Illustration. Abraham Lincoln used to tell the story of a man who heated a piece of iron in a forge, not knowing just what he was going to make out of it. At first he thought he would make a horseshoe. Then he changed his mind and thought he would make something else. After he had hammered on this design for a little while, he changed his mind and started hammering something else. By this time, he had so hammered the iron that it wasn't good for much of anything. Holding it up with his tongs, and looking at it in disgust, the blacksmith thrust it hissing into a tub of water. "Well, at least I can make a fizzle out of it!" he exclaimed.

One of the points that I want to make today is that it is easy for us to get caught up in ambitions that will have no eternal value. Today we are talking about work-

working hard at our relationship with Christ. However, it is quite easy to work on the things in life that are just going to fizzle out.

Ask someone to read 1 Corinthians 3:11-15 aloud.

Emphasize these points—

(1) In order for us to grow and mature in Christ, we must make a commitment to the things in life that are going to last. Christ—not things, or other people—must be our solid foundation in order for us to grow spiritually. Everything revolves around Christ. Our lives must orbit around Him and His plans for us.

(2) Personal growth in Christ requires a passion to make Christ the "XL supersized Master" of our lives.
Mini-illustration. Imagine Christ sitting in the McDonald's drive-thru window of your life. You place your order, "A powerful passion for Christ, please. Oh, by the way, Jesus, *supersize it!*"

(3) Growth and maturity in Christ sometimes happens in the oddest places. Places like our times of persecution or suffering.

•*When have you known this to be true in your life? Why is this true?*

KEY CONCEPT #3:
We must work at giving Christ to each other externally.

Illustration. **Bring in five one-dollar bills, and give them out to five people. Ask these people how they would use that dollar if they had to spend it today.**

I could give you a number of things that would make your life momentarily richer. By giving you a dollar, that moment is shortlived—bigtime. But by giving you Christ, I am giving you something that makes you rich forever. In fact, I am giving you something/ someone that keeps on giving. It multiplies as it is continually given away.

HINT:

During your mini-lecture, work through the three Key Concepts as a facilitator. Encourage your participants to talk through these points with you; invite questions and/or comments as you go. Offer the concepts and the subpoints, then ask for discussion. Keeping the presentation open-ended in this way allows the group members to focus on their areas of concern—their agenda, rather than yours.

•*What does it mean, in practical terms, to give Christ to each other? What are some tangible ways than we can do that?*

Subpoints to emphasize:

(1) As we communicate and interact with each other, we must make a special effort to speak Christ's words to each other. Choose your words carefully. Are the words you speak mainly words of life, or words of death? Here are some examples:

"I love you."
"I don't like her."
"I am listening."
"I don't care."
"You are a quality person."
"What's your problem, anyway?"

(2) Remember, it's easy to give ourselves away to each other. But there is rarely any power in that gift. The power comes when we give away Christ, in little and large ways. It is Christ who impacts people's lives, not us! This is hard work, but so much more rewarding. What you want your friends to think after you have spent time with them is: I see Christ in you; thanks for giving me Christ!

Conclusion

Augustine was bishop in Africa in the fifth century. He said, "Christ is not valued at all—unless He is valued above all." Let's work hard to make and build a community where Christ is valued above all. Not just in some lives, or in some things, or in some ways. But in each one of our lives, in each one of our souls.

We can do this by changing every day for Christ, from the inside out. Our private world is where it all starts. It is then communicated by our passion and drive for continued growth and maturity, our desire to be an "impact player" for God. It is then wrapped up in giving Christ to each other.

When we can put these attitudes and actions into place, a powerful phenomenon will happen in this community. Jesus will be seen, heard, and felt...and that is what it's all about!

GOING DEEPER

Fun with the Greek—

•**Christ / *christos*.** The Greek word means "anointed," translated as Messiah, a term applied to the priests who were anointed with the holy oil, particularly the High Priest (see Lev. 4:3, 5, 16). The single title *Christos* is sometimes used without the article to refer to the man Jesus, signifying the One who by His Spirit and power indwells believers and molds their character in conformity to His likeness (see Rom. 8:10; Gal. 2:20; 4:19; Eph. 3:17).

•**Grow / *auxano*.** The Greek word meaning "to increase" refers to the growth of that which lives, naturally or spiritually. It is often used to signify the effect of the work of God (see 1 Cor. 3:6, 7; 2 Cor. 9:10).

EXTRA OPTIONS

Pick and Choose any of the following to fit the needs of your group...

Options to Consider...for Step 1

Air Race

Needed: One balloon per person, plus a few extras for those pops; markers, and a prize music CD.

This is a race using a deflating balloon. Begin by handing out balloons to everyone. Have them write their names on the balloons with felt-tip markers. Line everyone up on one end of the room and have participants blow up their balloons (but not tie them). Tell them this is a race and that the winner gets a new music CD. The race begins with everyone holding up the balloon and then releasing it, watching closely where it lands. "Run to it, blow it up again, until you reach the other side of the room (i.e., when the balloon hits the wall). The first balloon to hit the wall wins. After a declaring a winner, ask:

• *When have you been the most "deflated" by failing to reach a goal (or having someone stop you)? What did this do to your ambition?*

Blind Polygon

Safety Note: If anyone has a bad back, he or she may want to sit this one out!

In this activity, everyone sits in a circle with their feet out in front of them. Each person is to cross arms and grab the person's hand on both sides. Then tell the group to try and stand up *all together*. If the group fails, encourage them to try again so that everyone comes up together. Then discuss:

• *What things are easy to do together in this group? What is difficult?*
• *How can individual spiritual growth contribute to a group's sense of togetherness?*

Options to Consider...for Step 3

Makin' A Change for Christ—Have two people do the old "Small People" skit with a sheet, table, and any props you choose. To set the stage for the skit, make a slit in the sheet at waist level and hang the sheet so it covers the person behind and also the front of the table. The person whose face will be seen, slides his/her arms through a pair of pants and the hands go into shoes. The person behind the sheet slides his/her arms through the sleeves of the front person's shirt.

The skit could be focused around "ambition for Christ" but starting with all the wrong areas: like looks, income, talents, and then coming to the conclusion that it is the heart that must change. End with a prayer of submission. There is great power in hard laughter and then spoken truth. Have fun!

Object Lesson—Use clay and soft black dirt. Illustrate how God wants us to be ready for change in our lives, but He must be free to move. Here are some different ideas to use: the Holy Spirit is a worm free to go through the dirt; rocks are sin; fertilizer is the Word of God.

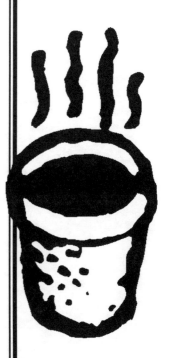

Mime fun—Call two or three people one week before the session. Ask them to develop a skit around the theme of "Giving Christ Away."

Options to Consider...for Step 4

"We Could..."—Have everyone get into small groups and ask participants to listen to situations that you will read to them. Each group should then talk about the problem and how they, as an individual and/or team, would "give away Christ" in the situation.

   Situation #1: A young girl in the youth group has just come to church for the first time in over four months. She is six months pregnant and staying close to her parents.

   Situation #2: A new woman has entered your Sunday Morning Singles Class. During the sharing time, she tells the group that she has just had a baby, but her boyfriend doesn't help very much with watching it. She finds it difficult to do anything with the singles group because of time constraints.

   Situation #3: An older man down the street from the church walks by every morning before the service. He walks very awkwardly and pushes an old shopping cart. Everyone in the singles group has seen him on their way into the church.

Options to Consider...for Step 5

Pain Partners—Encourage people to partner up with someone they are comfortable with and either share their pain from the past or simply leave it as an unspoken prayer request. Then have them pray for each other.

Jesus at the Super Bowl—For the first time in history, the guy at the Super Bowl holding the John 3:16 poster will not be at the game—because he gave you his ticket. It is now your job to make a poster promoting ambition for Jesus Christ.

FIRE IN THE HOLE!

Everyone find a partner and place an inflated balloon between you. When the leader yells, "Fire in the Hole!" partners must attempt to pop the balloon by squeezing together. After the fun, discuss:

- *What are your primary ambitions? How will you know when you are a successful person?*
- *Have your high expectations of success in life ever "squeezed" you to the breaking point? Tell about it.*

WHADDAYA THINK?

- What do you see coworkers pursuing in life? How do their pursuits affect you?
- To what extent do you evaluate your relationship with God on: how well you perform?
- What are the advantages and problems with daily spiritual disciplines?
- In your opinion, how could individual "spiritual ambition" contribute to the strengthening of community in this group?

KEY CONCEPTS
on Your Eternal Ambition

Though salvation comes only by the grace of God, growing in Christ is the greatest ambition we can have. So let's—

#1 Work at _____ing for Christ—_____ally.

#2 Work at _____ing and maturing in Christ—_____ally.

#3 Work at _____ing Christ to each other— _____ally.

INCOMPLETE COMPLETIONS

Finish the following statements (in private):

1. The one thing from the past that continues to haunt me is

_____.

2. _____ has caused me the

most pain in the past year.

3. _____ has really given me a passion

to grow for Christ.

4. God is calling me to suffer for Christ by _____.

5. I need to let go of _____ for the sake of Christ.

For no one can lay any foundation other than the one already laid, which is Jesus Christ. 12 If any man builds on this foundation using gold, silver, costly stones, wood, hay or straw, 13 his work will be shown for what it is, because the Day will bring it to light. It will be revealed with fire, and the fire will test the quality of each man's work. 14 If what he has built survives, he will receive his reward. 15 If it is burned up, he will suffer loss; he himself will be saved, but only as one escaping through the flames.
—1 Corinthians 3:11-15

But whatever was to my profit I now consider loss for the sake of Christ. 8 What is more, I consider everything a loss compared to the surpassing greatness of knowing Christ Jesus my Lord, for whose sake I have lost all things. I consider them rubbish, that I may gain Christ.
—Philippians 3:7-8

1 TON

For no one can lay any foundation other than the one already laid, which is Jesus Christ. 12 If any man builds on this foundation using gold, silver, costly stones, wood, hay or straw, 13 his work will be shown for what it is, because the Day will bring it to light. It will be revealed with fire, and the fire will test the quality of each man's work. 14 If what he has built survives, he will receive his reward. 15 If it is burned up, he will suf-fer loss; he himself will be saved, but only as one escaping through the flames.

—1 Corinthians 3:11-15

But whatever was to my profit I now consider loss for the sake of Christ. 8 What is more, I consider everything a loss compared to the surpassing greatness of knowing Christ Jesus my Lord, for whose sake I have lost all things. I consider them rubbish, that I may gain Christ.

—Philippians 3:7-8

INTERACT—AMBITIOUS...OR NOT?

When it comes to ambition, I'd have to say that I'm a...

- ___**Slug.** Just let me lay here, please.
- ___**Ostrich.** I prefer not to look, 'cause everybody's passing me by.
- ___**Turtle.** Slowly, but surely, I'll make my goals.
- ___**Octopus.** I'm branching out in many directions, with a "stick to it" attitude.
- ___**Piranha.** Outta my way, or I'll gobble you up.
- ___**Racehorse.** I'm galloping along toward the finish line.
- ___**Tasmanian Devil.** Gotta keep moving, no matter what!

•*Tell the other group members why you chose your particular response.*
•*How would you rate your ambition for spiritual growth compared to your ambition for success in the world?*

KEY CONCEPTS
On Your Eternal Ambition

Though salvation comes only by the grace of God, growing in Christ is the greatest ambition we can have. So let's—

#1 Work at _____ing for Christ—_____ally.

#2 Work at _____ing and maturing in Christ—_____ally.

#3 Work at _____ing Christ to each other—_____ally.

VULNERABILITY INVENTORY

Everyone find a partner and respond/discuss:

When I hear the call to "be more real" with the people in this group, I know that I need...

- ____ to be more sure that it would be safe to reveal my inner world.
- ____ to know that others will respond in similar ways.
- ____ to close up a little; I've already been too vulnerable.
- ____ to heal from past wounds first.
- ____ to set boundaries first. I'm too willing to "spill my guts."
- ____ to receive more courage from the Lord, in order to start opening up.
- ____ other: _____.

Take Home Page ABC

TIME FOR A RESPONSE

The most personally relevant thing I've learned in this session is:

AMBITION SELF-EVALUATOR...

Jot down brief responses to see how ambition has affected your life so far.

•Most of my thoughts about the future focus on ...

•When I think about the idea of spending a whole week "just relaxing" I become ....

•If I were to put my "life's dream" into one sentence, it would read ...

•The level of enjoyment I get from "striving for a goal" is ...

•As I look back over my life, I can see that my level of ambition has caused...

QUOTE REACTIONS

You'll be assigned one of the four quotations in "In Other Words.". Then respond:

•*Do you agree or disagree with this statement? Why?*

•*What personal illustration from your life seems to affirm or deny this quote?*

•*How would you rewrite this quotation to make it more relevant to your unique experience?*

IN OTHER WORDS...

The most important aspect of Christianity is not the work we do, but the relationship we maintain and the surrounding influence and qualities produced by that relationship.
—Oswald Chambers, *My Utmost for His Highest*

It is not enough to be busy; so are the ants. The question is: What are we busy about?
— Henry David Thoreau

DAILY READINGS AND REFLECTIONS

Monday—Philippians 3:7-8. Paul proclaims that all things are a "loss compared to the surpassing greatness of knowing Christ Jesus my Lord." Do you know Christ this well? Pray for a deepened knowledge of Christ and to have the "fellowship of sharing in His sufferings."

Tuesday—Philippians 1:20-21. Paul says that for him to live is Christ. Compare your source of life's meaning to that of Paul's. Ask the Father for a greater courage to live for Christ every day.

Wednesday—John 21:21-22. Jesus reprimanded Peter to simply follow. Does spiritual maturity mean that we stop comparing ourselves with others? Pray for a greater ability to focus on following Jesus.

Thursday—1 Corinthians 10:31. God has called for your whole life to be sacrificed to Him. Where, in your life, can you work on glorifying God to a greater degree? Where do you need to "take out the weeds" and plant good seed?

Friday—Matthew 5:38-42. God has called you to love beyond what is expected. How can you flesh that out in your life? Pray for an awareness of how the Holy Spirit is at work and how you can be a part of His work.

Saturday—1 Corinthians 1:26-31. God has chosen you to be His "fool"! What does this mean to you? Ask God for humility and total reliance upon Jesus Christ for your sense of identity.

JUST FOR FUN

Consider doing these things on the spur of the moment with a desire simply to serve.

1. With a non-Christian. Take your friend to a rock-climbing gym and try a few climbs. Afterwards, share your concern about his or her life and how it is not "Belayed In" to Jesus Christ. Our souls need a harness and a rope too, and it is through Jesus's death that we are safe to climb.

2. For Single Parents. Talk with someone in the music department at a local school, or go to a music store, and let your child try playing a few different instruments. If you find one he or she likes to play, ask around the church and see if anyone plays that instrument. See if they would be willing to give a few introductory lessons. You may be starting a junior Beethoven on a great career path!

3. For Older Singles. Take a walk with a younger single and share about your life adventures with him or her. Let your younger friend ask you any question and encourage them in their singleness. Great opportunity to speak truth to younger men and women.

THINK—for Next Week: When have you experienced the joy of forgiveness?

Session 5
EVERYBODY NEEDS
Forgiveness

I (Joel) was just a kid of eight years old, and I really liked candy. So going into that little store on the corner and suddenly seeing rows and rows of candy bars, lemon drops, Tootsie Rolls, and peppermint sticks was just too much for me. I had to have some of it.

Just one candy bar...Yes!

Later, as I sat in the garage enjoying my stolen chocolate treasure, Dad walked in through the side door. I froze in a guilty daze as he asked where I got the money for that candy. After I retold my sinful escapade, Dad made me go back to the store, pay the cashier, and say, "I'm sorry, I was wrong for stealing the candy bar. Will you forgive me?"

It was excruciating, to say the least.

But it's a part of every life—messing up. Having to say "I'm sorry." Getting forgiven. That's why one of the greatest things you can do for your singles is to convince them to "go to the corner store with each other." Forgiveness is a foundational pillar of powerful community. It is even more powerful when it becomes a part of the everyday language that your singles speak to each other.

SESSION AIM

To help single adults embrace the vital role that forgiveness plays in healthy community.

WHAT'S IT ALL ABOUT?

In this session communicate the three Key Concepts below. Emphasize that forgiveness is a foundational pillar of powerful community. Therefore, we can...

• Embrace forgiveness as a vital part of our life together.
• Expect to fail each other, but deal with failure appropriately.
• Extend forgiveness, as an action prompted by a Christ-like attitude.

BIBLE REFERENCES:

Mark 11:25
Luke 17:4
Ephesians 4:32
Colossians 3:13

Your 'Short Course' Set-Up...

(How to Use This Material in 35-45 Minutes)

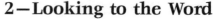

Example: Sunday Morning Bible Study

1—Let's Get Started
(5-10 minutes)

Option 1: To Get Forgiveness

This is a variation of the old television game, "To Tell the Truth." In advance, ask four people to be ready to stand up in front of the group. Each of the four must tell the group about a "childhood blunder." Here's the catch: three of the four tell a made-up story, and one tells the truth. The group votes on which one is "to get forgiveness" (by guessing the one who actually *needs* it). In other words, the only one that gets forgiveness is the one the group thinks is telling the truth!

Use this activity to begin a discussion along these lines:

•When was forgiveness the most beautiful gift you've received?

•How hard or easy is it for you to offer forgiveness to others? Can you share an example?

Option 2: Blundering Demonstrations

Split the entire group into teams of eight to ten. Have volunteers in each group act out (in charade fashion) a childhood blunder for the rest of the team. Have the team members try to guess what the blunder is. It would be good for the team leader to demonstrate her blunder to the team first. Then discuss:

•Why do childhood blunders stick in our minds? How does the reaction of significant adults affect our self-esteem later in life? Our image of God?

Option 3: Discussion Questions

Start your session with the activity on Interactive Page #1 titled "Forgiveness Inventory." Have participants form into pairs or small groups to discuss before reporting their insights to the larger group.

Note: If time or interest allows, use additional options found on pages 73-74.

2—Looking to the Word
(15 minutes)

Present the material found in "Presenting What the Bible Has to Say," on pages 70-72. Think through the outline and key points, and make the presentation your own by adding personal illustrations.

3—Applying It to My Life
(5-10 minutes)

As soon as you complete your presentation, have everyone move into small groups or pairs. Ask the groups to work through the discussion questions in the "Whaddaya Think?" section on Interactive page #1. After a few minutes, invite sharing of insights with the larger group.

4—Taking the Next Step
(5 minutes)

Needed: Paper and pencils.

Distribute paper and pencil to each individual and tell your singles it's time for a writing assignment. On the chalkboard or newsprint, write these instructions for everyone's response.

(1) List as many people as you can remember—who have forgiven you in the past. . .

(2) Jot a paragraph about the impact this forgiveness has had on you . . .

(3) Make a list of people whom you need to forgive (living or dead) . . .

(4) Write a paragraph, envisioning what impact it might have on them or you or future circumstances . . .

Ask your singles to keep these papers in their Bibles during the week, for review and reflection during their quiet times. Ask them to pray that God would give them the courage to take action in extending forgiveness to those who need it.

5—Let's Wrap It Up
(5 minutes)

1. Make any announcements for the coming week.

2. Lead the group in the song, "Amazing Grace," and then end in prayer.

HINT:

Remember that your transitions from one activity to the next should happen very quickly. Try to end an exercise right after group members are most involved. Don't let the activity die down before introducing the next one. Keep them wanting more time.

When You Have More Time...

(How to Use This Material in 60-90 Minutes)
Example: Small Groups at Home

1—Let's Get Started
(5-10 minutes)

Option 1: Human Camera

Pair up everyone and have them guide one another around the room or outdoor area, one at a time. One person places her hands on the shoulders of the other and proceeds to move him around the room—as he keeps his eyes closed (he'll be functioning as a "human camera"). During this time, whenever the guide taps her "camera" on the shoulder, he will blink his eyes and try to remember what he saw. After six pictures have been taken, stop and ask the "camera" to try to recall all of the pictures, in order. Switch roles, and then discuss:

•*How hard or easy is it for you to recall the times when grace and forgiveness has been extended to you?*
•*How can such recollections increase our "attitude of gratitude" in life? Our sense of close community? Can you share a personal example?*

Option 2: Grand Prix

Use the activity titled "Grand Prix" as described on Interactive Page #2.

Note: If time or interest allows, use additional options found on pages 73-74.

2—Looking to the Word
(20-25 minutes)

Present the material found in "Presenting What the Bible Has to Say," on pages 70-72. Divide your allotted time into three segments: (1) Introduction, (2) Key Concepts, and (3) Conclusion. Keep your presentation short and simple. Hit the highlights, drawing upon the "Going Deeper" information as appropriate.

3—Applying It to My Life
(10-15 minutes)

Once you complete your presentation, have everyone get started doing the "Interact" case study exercise on Interactive

page #2. Do the activity in triads, with each person taking on one of the roles (girl, counselor, pastor) in order to respond to the questions that follow.

4—Taking the Next Step
(15-20 minutes)

Needed: pencils or pens.

Distribute the Take-Home Page and have everyone work on the "Time for a Response" section. Encourage people to compare their responses and explain what they are going to do with them.

5—Let's Wrap It Up
(10-15 minutes)

1. Form a circle. Then have everyone bow their heads and offer a sentence prayer beginning with one of these phrases:

I praise You for Your...
I love You for Your...
Thank You for...

2. After the sentence prayers, make your group announcements and close in prayer.

HINT:

Following the "Grand Prix" activity, you can use the debriefing questions with everyone standing, facing each other. No need to go through all the questions; you judge which ones you like—or add your own. Just remember: Keep things moving and don't overdo the debriefing. Use the activity to move you into your mini-lecture in Step 2.

HINT:

During the case study discussion, let your singles know that they can play any role, regardless of their gender.

Extending The Learning...
(How to Use This Material in Two Hours)
Example: Extended Week-Night Program

HINT:

Be ready to make appointments during the week with any person(s) who wish to pursue the topic of forgiveness(and personal issues related to it)in private with you. Realize that this may raise a counseling opportunity for individuals' past hurts or conflicts among group members. Be prepared to refer to your pastor or other professional if/when the issues will require more than one or two sessions of directive work. Realize that for healing with severe abuse, this may require long-term therapy.

1—Let's Get Started
(20-30 minutes)

Option 1: Crazy Cures
Needed: *Pen and paper for each group.*

Form into groups of six to eight people. List these common ailments of the human race on the chalkboard: Common Cold, Flu, Back Ache, Nose Bleed, Ear Ache, Warts, Baldness, Soar Throat, Upset Stomach. Then have group members try to list as many known cures for the ailments as they can in five minutes. Give points to each group for every "unique" cure that no other group mentioned. Debrief with these questions:

•*What kinds of diseases can attack our souls, when we refuse to give or receive forgiveness? Do you have any personal experience or observations related to this?*

Option 2: Hypothetical Reactions
Direct your students to the "Hypothetical Reactions" activity on the Take Home Page. Give everyone a couple of minutes to think about how they would actually respond in the real-life situation. Then point to people and ask them to say it exactly as if you, the leader, were their neighbor.

2—Looking to the Word
(25 minutes)

Present the material found in "Presenting What the Bible Has to Say," on pages 70-72.

3—Applying It to My Life
(30-40 minutes)

Needed: *Butcher paper and marker.*

Use an acrostic activity for applying the biblical material. Tape a huge piece of butcher paper to the wall and jot these capital letters, vertically, down the left-hand side:

F O R G I V I N G   H E R E

Tell group members that their task is to fill in the acrostic by coming up with words or phrases that tell: what kinds of things need to happen in this group if conflicts are to be resolved, forgiveness is to be

extended, grace is to permeate the atmosphere. Stress that the ideas should be practical and relevant to your group.

4—Taking the Next Step
(20-30 minutes)

Needed: *Loaves of french bread.*

Tell your group that some of the ideas they've suggested could be put into practice right now, before the close of the meeting. So hold a "Love Feast," based on the acrostic you've just completed. Break off chunks of bread for each individual. Tell everyone that in a moment they will go to each of the other group members, offering a piece of their bread and taking a piece. Each will say to the other: "I love you, and . . ."

Participants can complete the statement with any of these options (jot them on the chalkboard)—
- a word of affirmation and/or affection
- an honest criticism or complaint (but using "I" statements; e.g.: "I'm still feeling hurt by a comment you made . . .")
- an expression of past hurts or present conflict
- a request for an apology
- a request to be forgiven

Stress that this is a time for listening intently and trying to feel what the other person is feeling. No arguing, but seeking to understand—moving toward forgiveness and reconciliation wherever it is needed.

5—Let's Wrap It Up
(5 minutes)

1. Sing a praise song, holding hands.
2. Do a "group hug" and close in prayer.

My Personal Game Plan ABC

STEP 1   Time: _____ minutes.

Materials Needed:

Activities Summary:

STEP 2   Time: _____ minutes.

Materials Needed:

Activities Summary:

STEP 3   Time: _____ minutes.

Materials Needed:

Activities Summary:

STEP 4   Time: _____ minutes.

Materials Needed:

Activities Summary:

STEP 5   Time: _____ minutes.

Materials Needed:

Activities Summary:

Just for You
Teacher's Devotional

I can't remember who said it, but it's one of the better quotations jotted into my journal. Maybe it will inspire you, too:

How can we gain a forgiving heart? Only by going to the Cross and there seeing how much our Lord has forgiven us and at what a cost. Then we shall see that the utmost we are called upon to forgive, compared with what we have been forgiven, is a very little thing.

As leaders caught in the trenches of battle, we can forget that the focus of all our activity, the motivation for all our work, the goal of every meeting is . . . the Cross! To remember it, to preach it, to appropriate its power in our lives. That power stems from the forgiveness it has won for us. As the Scripture says: "He forgave us all our sins, having canceled the written code, with its regulations, that was against us and that stood opposed to us; he took it away, nailing it to the cross" (Col. 2:13b-14).

If you were to go to the Cross right now and extend forgiveness to certain individuals, who would those people be? Going to the Cross is like securing a room with a view. It is your opportunity as a leader to see in full color what Christ has done for you. Then you can act upon what you've seen!

—Joel and Kent

MY GOALS FOR THIS SESSION:

- TO HELP SINGLE ADULTS

_____
_____
_____

- TO HELP SINGLE ADULTS

_____
_____
_____

- TO HELP SINGLE ADULTS

_____
_____
_____

- TO HELP SINGLE ADULTS

_____
_____
_____

WHAT I LEARNED FROM READING 'LOOKING TO THE WORD' . . .

Notes and Insights—

Presenting
What the Bible Has to Say...

H ere's your mini-lecture covering the biblical Key Concepts. Try to become familiar with the flow of thoughts, and the outline, in order to present this material with maximum eye contact. Special instructions to you are in bold type. (Note: Have group members refer to the Key Concepts section on their Interactive Page. They may wish to fill in the blanks as you speak.)

Introduction

In advance, conduct some "man on the street" interviews with people in your church or community. Have each person answer the three questions below on cassette tape. Then begin your presentation by playing the tape to your group.

Question #1: Define forgiveness.
Question #2: If forgiveness were a color, what color would it be, and why?
Question #3: If forgiveness were a sound, what kind of sound would it be? Why?

THE KEY CONCEPTS

Transition statement: Some of us probably understand forgiveness better than others. It often depends on the family we grew up in. If forgiveness was modeled there, valued and taught there, then it may be a little easier for us to know what it entails. However, I think many of us underestimate the power that real forgiveness can have on a group like ours. If we, as a body, would embrace and model forgiveness in our relationships, God would rain down unbelievable blessing on us.

Let's take some time today to discover what it means to be a group that practices forgiveness. After all, forgiveness is a foundational pillar of powerful community. Therefore, we can...

•Embrace forgiveness as a vital part of our life together.

•Expect to fail each other, but deal with failure appropriately.
•Extend forgiveness, as an action prompted by a Christlike attitude.

KEY CONCEPT #1:
Embrace forgiveness as a vital part of our life together.

Illustration. **"Didn't Want to Let Go." Tell the group of a time when you really embraced someone that you love. It could be a friend or relative, maybe when you saw them again after many years of distance, or when you put them on a plane to go back home. Tell them about the event in detail. Tell them how you felt when you embraced your friend/relative. Were there tears of joy?**

In the same way that I embraced my friend physically, we as individuals must embrace (to clasp in the arms lovingly, hug, accept readily) forgiveness in our group. Paul talks about embracing forgiveness in Colossians 3:13.

Have someone read this verse aloud. Then offer these subpoints about the nature of forgiveness:

(1) It is a sign of strength. One of the main reasons why so many communities are dysfunctional, is because of their unwillingness to embrace forgiveness. Many people feel that forgiveness is a sign of weakness, but it really is a sign of strength.

(2) It can be a part of our "love language." If we embrace forgiveness, we in essence are valuing it and modeling it to each other. Because of this, forgiveness becomes a part of the love language that we speak to each other.

(3) It escalates relationship. Embracing forgiveness is saying to one another, and to our team, that we are willing to be vulnerable and real with each other. When teams can be vulnerable and real with each other, relationships will always escalate.

KEY CONCEPT #2:
Expect to fail each other, but deal with failure appropriately.

Illustration. **"Expectation Card."** Pull an expectation card out of your wallet or purse. Tell the group that you plan to carry this card wherever you go. On the card are certain behaviors, actions, or attitudes that you're going to expect out of the people you'll encounter on a daily basis. For example, you'll expect: **friendliness, kindness, honesty, helpfulness, encouragement.**

Then point out that one of your expectations, as you get to know people, is...failure.

As we enter into relationship with each other, all of us have our expectation cards in hand. You may not actually carry a card around like this one. But more than likely you have an expectation checklist in your head. We definitely expect others to act in certain ways and sometimes to "perform" according to certain expectations. However, one of the actions that we least expect is failure. Let's look at Luke 17:4:

Subpoints to emphasize:

(1) In Luke 17, we find that Jesus has his own expectation card. He expects and understands that His followers will fail.

•*Why do you think that is so important as we relate to each other?*

(2) Forgiveness can only occur when we as a team *expect* to fail one another. It's going to happen. And if it is handled properly, it can be one of the most positive things that can happen in our relationships. How could it be positive?

The answer is that people experience tremendous freedom—at work, in families, in the church—when they know they are allowed to fail. This causes everyone to be real with each other. It helps us grow and learn from our mistakes. And it forces us to extend grace to each other in our mutually recognized weaknesses.

Offer a couple cool quotations at this time:

Not failure, but low aim, is crime.—James Russell Lowell

Man takes account of our failures, but God of our striving.—Unknown

KEY CONCEPT #3:
Extend forgiveness, as an action prompted by a Christlike attitude.

Illustration. **Bring in a vacuum cleaner. Make sure that it has some of the available extensions, especially the one used for cleaning in corners. Attach the corner extension, turn on the vacuum, and clean some of the corners of the room.**

Forgiveness is a lot like this corner extension. In order to make forgiveness happen, or to display it in our relationships, we must put on the "extension"—and take action. That is, forgiveness is something we must purposefully extend to each other. It is getting into the corners of each others' lives and doing some cleaning. This can readily occur when we are all desiring to be like Christ with each other.

Now read Ephesians 4:32 aloud and make these two points:

(1) Possessing a Christlike attitude means having a forgiving spirit. One of the very real reason that we commit to forgive each other is because of the awesome fact that Christ has, and continues to forgive each of us. Jesus knows what kind of people we are....sinners. Yet, he is willing to pull out the vacuum and continually extend forgiveness to us.

(2) Forgiveness takes work. To extend forgiveness means to work at forgiveness. To make it work in our relationships with each other. It doesn't just happen. It happens when we make it happen.

Conclusion

Forgiveness is one of the most powerful gifts we offer to each other in community. When exercised properly, it is a most effective tool for making us one in spirit. Think about this: forgiveness is one of the foundational clues that God really lives in each of us. It lets others know that we love Christ and want to live for Him.

So...Who are the people in your life that you just can't forgive? Maybe it is something they've said or done to you. Is it Dad, Mom, Stepdad, Stepmom, a friend, a fellow employee, or maybe someone right here in this room? Christ is honored when we, His people, obey His words.

To forgive doesn't mean that we don't hold a person accountable for his actions. It doesn't mean forgetting about the hurt or ignoring the pain he has caused us. We still have to work through all of that, perhaps with counseling, over the years.

Forgiving simply means releasing ourselves from the burden of hatred, no matter how the other person responds—even if that person refuses to acknowledge our forgiveness (or if that person is no longer living).

As long as we harbor animosity, we are letting the other person's wrongdoing bind us up in the chains of bitterness. It is our choice to lay down those chains...and be free.

GOING DEEPER

Forgiveness is a command. We are commanded to forgive. Forget the injury, never think of it again. We are to repeat this every time he repeats his sin. Christians should be of a forgiving spirit, willing to think the best of everybody, and they should seek as much to show that they have forgiven an injury as others do to show that they resent it.
—*Matthew Henry*

Other Forgiveness topics and verses—
• A forgiving God (Ex. 34:7; Num. 14:18; Ps. 86:5; 1 John 1:9).
• Forgiving humans (Prov. 17:9; Gen. 50:17; 1 Sam. 25:28; Ex. 10:17).
• Forgiveness by repentance (Mark 1:4; Luke 3:3; Acts 2:38; Acts 3:19).
• Forgive one another (Matt. 18:1-2; Mark 11:25; 2 Cor. 2:7; 2 Cor. 2:10).

Excellent Illustration. In a recent chapel service bulletin from Chaplain Wendell C. Hawley, comes a classic illustration of forgiveness. When the Moravian missionaries first went to the Eskimos, they couldn't find a word in the Eskimo language for forgiveness. So they had to make a compound word from other words. It turned out to be: *Issumagijoujungnainermik.* This is a formidable looking assembly of letters, but an expression that has a beautiful connotation for those who understand it. It means: "Not-being-able-to-think-about-it-anymore."

you are here

EXTRA OPTIONS

Pick and Choose any of the following to fit the needs of your group...

Options to Consider...for Step 1

Jump

Needed: One long jump rope for each group.

Have two people take different ends of the rope and start to twirl at a slow pace. Have small groups compete by getting people on their teams through without touching the rope. If anyone touches, the whole teams must start over. If this is too easy, you may speed up the rope or try to get the whole team jumping at once. Use this activity to teach forgiveness—when the whole team must start over because of one member's failure.

Impossible Build

Needed: One deck of cards for each group.

The object is for small groups to compete by building the tallest structure with playing cards. Have each team try to build the tallest structure possible with the deck of cards. You can leave it to chance or you can do the damage yourself, but have a structure fall "accidently." Obviously, you will make the big request afterwards, "Please forgive me?"

Toxic Waste

Needed: Five pieces of string, each six feet long, per team; a rubber band; a Dixie cup with water in it; a vase.

In advance, do this set-up: Put the vase about 20 feet away from the disposable cup. Place plastic or towels underneath the cup and the vase. Fill the disposable cup with water.

Form teams and give each team five pieces of string. Tell the teams they must not come within three feet of the water at any time because it is toxic! The idea is to move the toxic waste (water) from the cup to the vase using only the pieces of string. No knots allowed, and one person must be on each end of the string.

Alternative: You may make this challenge more involved by making it "bigger." For example: use rope, trash cans or buckets, and colored water or even real sludge. Remember to guard for clean up. Use plastic and newspaper wherever possible. The more creative the materials, the greater the involvement will be. Eventually, follow up with questions like these:

- **What things in this experience were vital to group success?**
- **How is toxic waste like inner pain that others have caused us?**
- **How did we fail each other in this experience? How did we handle our failures?**
- **Is it possible to disregard forgiving someone, and just go on living?**
- **Is forgiveness an everyday issue? How? Why?**

Options to Consider...for Step 3

Touched by Forgiveness—Have everyone imagine a new TV show called "Touched By Forgiveness," which has called for a new show script. Your group must write a story involving someone who "messes up big time" but is restored back to faith by a group of caring friends.

73

Moving Movie—Show the powerful movie "The Mission" and have a discussion on the impact one individual's experience of forgiveness may have on a whole community. (Preview the movie first—to judge appropriateness, and to develop relevant discussion questions.)

Options to Consider...for Step 4

Just Do It!—Commit to going to one person during the coming week who you may have sinned against. Ask for their forgiveness.

Campfire Sharing—Meet in a place where you can all sit near a fireplace or campfire. Campfires always create an environment for deeper sharing. Invite a few people to share about some key experiences in their lives with forgiveness. How are they doing now?

Advertising Forgiveness—Make posters that can be held on the curb side by the singles group. These will be signs that promote the idea of honesty and forgiveness. Choose a Saturday afternoon when the singles can get together and have a picnic. But before the picnic starts, have everyone grab a sign and go stand by the road. Watch the smiles and waves—especially when people find out you are not offering a car wash!

Options to Consider...for Step 5

Partner Prayers—Offer prayers, with a partner, related to the topic of stubbornness in your lives. First think about how the Israelites continually refused to obey God—but He outloved them. Ask the Lord for a broken heart in the things you are most stubborn about. And, if possible, set up a means of accountability with your prayer partner for the month ahead.

God as Parent—Think of a personal instance in which you avoided the wrath of your parents as a child. Tell about the extent you went to avoid getting in trouble. Then read Psalm 130 out of *The Message* and compare the Lord's unfailing love with that of your parents.

FORGIVENESS INVENTORY

Think back through your past year. On the chart below, jot down the names of people that come to mind, related to each of the three categories—

I've Confronted	**I've Forgiven**	**I've Received Forgiveness From**

Now consider:

•*Are there people in your life whom you find it hard to love—because of their sin? Because of your sin?*

KEY CONCEPTS
on Forgiveness

Forgiveness is a foundational pillar of community. Therefore, we can...

#1 _____ forgiveness as a _____ of our life together.

#2 Expect to _____, and deal with failure

appropriately.

#3 _____ forgiveness, as an action prompted by _____.

WHADDAYA THINK?
- •In your opinion, what is the most difficult thing about the command to forgive?
- •How is corporate forgiveness related to individual forgiveness?
- •What is your typical attitude toward someone who has obviously sinned? sinned against you?
- •Do we need to forget the wrong that was done in order to forgive the wrongdoer? Explain.
- •Is it easier for you to forgive yourself or to forgive someone else? Why?
- •How would it help us if we truly believed that Christians—naturally—will fail each other? Can you give an example?

BIBLE TEXT

And when you stand praying, if you hold anything against anyone, forgive him, so that your Father in heaven may forgive you your sins.
—Mark 11:25

If he sins against you seven times in a day, and seven times comes back to you and says, "I repent," forgive him.
—Luke 17:4

Be kind and compassionate to one another, forgiving each other, just as in Christ God forgave you.
—Ephesians 4:32

Bear with each other and forgive whatever grievances you may have against one another,. Forgive as the Lord forgave you
—Colossians 3:13

And when you stand praying, if you hold anything against anyone, forgive him, so that your Father in heaven may forgive you your sins.
—**Mark 11:25**

If he sins against you seven times in a day, and seven times comes back to you and says, "I repent," forgive him.
—**Luke 17:4**

Be kind and compassionate to one another, forgiving each other, just as in Christ God forgave you.
—**Ephesians 4:32**

Bear with each other and forgive whatever grievances you may have against one another,. Forgive as the Lord forgave you
—**Colossians 3:13**

INTERACT

It's your first week at camp, serving as a cabin counselor for twelve teenaged girls. While everyone has gone to breakfast, one of the girls, Sarah, comes to you and says: "I've never told anyone this before, but it's making me so depressed. My father molested me from the age of seven until I was ten. Sometimes I feel like I want to kill myself—like I'm so guilty. Other times, I imagine killing him! What can I do? I suppose I should just forgive him. But I think I'd rather die."

Sarah begins to cry as she pleads with you to help her. As you open your mouth to respond, you're still wondering exactly what to say and do...

- As the counselor, describe your feelings. What are the first words that come out of your mouth?
- Be Sarah. When you hear teachings about "forgiveness," what happens inside you?
- What role might the Scriptures play in this situation? (See, for instance Ephesians 4:32.)
- Be Sarah's pastor. The counselor has told you of Sarah's case. What steps will you take?

OPENER IDEA: GRAND PRIX!

Each person find a partner. One of the partners is blindfolded, and he or she is referred to as "the car." The other partner then stands behind the car, and is "the driver." The driver goes through a series of non-verbal signals in order to guide the car:

- A touch on the right shoulder = RIGHT TURN.
- A touch on the left shoulder = LEFT TURN.
- Both hands "off" of the car = GO FORWARD.
- Both hands "on" = STOP!
- A repeated tapping on the car's back = BACK UP
- A repeated tapping on the head = HONKING THE HORN.

The cars must be driven through the entire room. The idea is NOT to touch anything with your car, especially another car or driver, as they travel. After a while, the partner's switch positions! You may want to increase the level of difficulty by limiting the size of the driving range. It definitely becomes more intense.

Warning: This is a trust activity. No joking around! (Variation: For smaller groups, you can use chairs or tables as obstacles for the cars to drive around.)

1. On a scale of one to ten (ten being the best) how well did you trust your driver?
2. What were the things that helped or hindered your trust of your driver?
3. How natural is it for us to trust one another with things that really matter?
4. What are some "accidental bumps" we've experienced as a result of others' failures? What role does forgiveness play at these times?

Take Home Page ABC

(CONTIUES FLIPSIDE)

TIME FOR A RESPONSE

The most personally relevant thing I've learned in this session is:

What can I do to put feet to this principle this week?

In my personal life:

In my church/personal ministry:

In my community:

In my workplace:

In my friendships:

THE NEXT STEP

Why Not Some Good News?—Write an article for your local newspaper on an act of forgiveness done in your community. This may take a little investigative reporting, but the outcome may be very beneficial.

HYPOTHETICAL REACTIONS

Suppose a neighbor were to say to you, with tears in her eyes: "The idea of forgiving people is way overrated—especially by all these sweetness-and-light Christians. There's a few people who've done some pretty horrible things to me. I mean, what am I supposed to do? Just forget about it and go on my merry way?"

What would you say? *Really!*

_____

_____

_____

_____

_____

_____

IN OTHER WORDS ...

Three fantastic quotes from Lewis B. Smedes, in *Forgive and Forget* (New York: Simon and Schuster, Inc., 1984).

As we forgive people, we gradually come to see the deeper truth about them, a truth our hate blinds us to, a truth we can see only when we separate them from what they did to us. When we heal our memories we are not playing games, we are not making believe. We see the truth again. For the truth about those who hurt us is that they are weak, needy, and fallible human beings. They were people before they hurt us and they are people after they hurt us.

Forgiveness: You know it has started when you begin to wish that person well.

(CONTIUES FLIPSIDE)

Take Home Page

DAILY READINGS AND REFLECTIONS

Monday—Read 2 Corinthians 5:10. Paul here talks about the coming judgment seat of Christ, which demands experienced forgiveness. How prepared are you for this coming day?

Tuesday—Read 1 Corinthians 3:3. Paul highlights the war being waged against the body of Christ. In what ways are you actively fighting the battle?

Wednesday—Read 1 John 2:2. God's forgiveness isn't just for us Christians but for the whole world. How could you spread this message a little better in your daily life?

Thursday—Read John 3:16. God gave up His own Son so we could experience forgiveness. Are you enjoying this restored relationship with God on a daily basis? How?

Friday—Read Isaiah 6:5. Isaiah realizes that he has sinned with his lips. What body parts would you name as most troubling and tempted?

Saturday—Read Acts 26:17-18. The basis of Christianity is receiving forgiveness of sins. In what creative ways can we communicate this message to others today?

RANDOM ACTS OF KINDNESS

Random acts of kindness are best done on the spur of the moment. Make them an experience that lasts a lifetime.

1. For parents: Write an appreciation card, recalling a specific instance in which your parents left a permanent impression of their love for you. Just for fun, ask for forgiveness for something that they may have never known about. That broken vase? Or the mysterious dent in the family car?

2. For nieces and nephews: Take them sledding or to the beach. Make the day a time of "loving on them." Afterwards, get an ice-cream cake with the message "I love you guys!" on it. These are things they will never forget.

3. For single parents of an older child: Take your son or daughter out for ice cream and bring up your desire to have an honest relationship with them. It may be necessary for you to demonstrate this by opening up to them. Discuss how important forgiveness is to you and the place it has in your relationship. This is setting the foundation for truth.

4. For non-Christian friends: Suggest that they read the book *Left Behind* by Jerry Jenkins and Tim La Haye. Then do a follow up ice-cream date raising the key question: "Will you be left behind?"

GETTING CLOSER

Consider taking your group on a High Adventure Trip. Arrange through a nearby outfitter or camp to spend a few days in the woods either backpacking, rock climbing, rappelling, mountain biking, rafting, or skiing. This would create the perfect environment for people to work on relationships without any distractions. You could give Peak 3 Outfitters a call in Colorado Springs: "800-GO-PEAK-3." We would love to put together a whole package for you, which would include a ministry, food, and the adventure. Leave all the details to us.

THINK—for Next Week: How do you rate yourself when it comes to encouraging others?

IN OTHER WORDS ...

Forgiving is tough. Excusing is easy. What a mistake it is to confuse forgiving with being mush, soft, gutless, and oh, so understanding. Before we forgive, we stiffen our spine and we hold a person accountable. And only then, with tough-minded judgment, can we do the outrageously impossible thing: we can forgive.

A Zealous and
OUTRAGEOUS
Encouragement

"All I get at work is one put-down after another," said Carlos. "I'm getting pretty tired of it. When I come to this singles group, I expect it to be different. I mean, if Christians can't be encouraging to one another, who can?"

Someone has said that for every negative comment you make to a person, you must make ten positive comments in order to just balance things out. That's a small indication of the kind of world we all live in. There's so much more tearing down than building up. It seems everyone's looking for ways to get ahead, at the expense of everyone else.

It's got to be different in the church! It's time to pull together.

Yes, the power of encouragement must flow as you minister to singles. They want, value, and need a team of individuals who are willing to believe in them and are able to build them up. This kind of support structure, especially for single adults, is a crucial requirement of their daily social diet. When you can get your singles to embrace the ministry of encouragement in each other's lives, true community will surface.

SESSION AIM

To help single adults understand that each one of them plays a vital "believer" and "builder" role in the ongoing spiritual development of their singles group.

WHAT'S IT ALL ABOUT?

This session offers two Key Concepts to communicate to your singles. When we embrace the ministry of encouragement, true community surfaces. Therefore, let us—

• Zealously believe in one another.
• Outrageously build up one another.

BIBLE REFERENCES:

Hebrews 10:24-25
1 Thessalonians 5:11

79

1—Let's Get Started
(5-10 minutes)

Option 1: Hula-Tube Competition
Needed: Either a Hula Hoop or a large inner tube for two groups.

Have your singles form two circles, with everyone holding hands. Place an inner tube on the arm of one of the members in each circle, and tell the group: "Move the inner tube around the circle by passing your whole body through the tube." Have the groups compete for the best time (complete two practice runs first). Offer a prize. Then ask:

•*Recall: What words of encouragement did you hear during this competition? What words of discouragement, or put-downs, did you hear (don't name names!)?*

Option 2: Whaddaya Think?
Start your session using the questions on Interactive Page #1, under "Whaddaya Think?" Have participants form pairs or small groups to discuss before reporting their insights to the larger group.

Note: If time or interest allows, use additional options found on pages 87-88.

2—Looking to the Word
(15 minutes)

Present the material found in "Presenting What the Bible Has to Say," on pages 84-86. Divide your allotted time into three segments: (1) Introduction, (2) Key Concepts, and (3) Conclusion. Keep your presentation short and direct.

3—Applying It to My Life
(5-10 minutes)

As soon as you complete your presentation, direct attention to the "When I Really Need It" portion of Interactive Page #1. Distribute pencils, and ask individuals to work in silence as they complete this ranking exercise.

4—Taking the Next Step
(5 minutes)

Now discuss (as a whole group, or in small groups) the question that follows the ranking exercise—

•*One way this group can help fill my need for encouragement is ...*

5—Let's Wrap It Up
(5 minutes)

1. Take any ideas that came out of the Step 4 sharing above, and commit to trying to implement at least one of them. Talk together about how you will do it. Be sure to stress that during this discussion, everyone should try to envision what it actually means, in practical terms, to *believe in one another* and to *build up one another.*

2. If you'll have time, share in pairs:

•*What is the greatest, most moving "encouragement event" you've ever experienced?*

Then pray together, asking God to give you an opportunity to be a part of someone else's greatest encouraging experience.

3. Make your group's announcements at this time.

4. Distribute the Take Home Page and close in prayer.

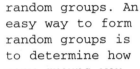
HINT:

To help singles get to know new people, form random groups. An easy way to form random groups is to determine how many groups you want and have participants number off consecutively from 1 to that number. Form groups of those with matching numbers. Allow extra time for relocating.

When You Have More Time...

(How to Use This Material in 60-90 Minutes)

Example: Small Groups at Home

1—Let's Get Started
(15-20 minutes)

Option 1: Blind Sizing

Tell the group that their task is to line up by shoe size—with eyes closed. When they get everyone in order, do a big group hug. Then, speaking of "sizes," ask—

•*When have you been cut down to size by someone? How did you feel? What did you do?*
•*When have you been built up by someone? Tell about it . . .*
•*How big a "feat" (pun intended) is it for you to be encouraging to fellow employees? to other Christians? to close friends? to parents or children?*
•*Why is it easy or difficult for you?*

Option 2: Up-N-Over
Needed: One rope for each group of eight to ten people.

The challenge here is to get all group members over a five-foot high rope without anyone touching it. This is a physically demanding activity! Tie a rope between to stationary points at about five-feet high, depending on the physical ability of the group. Inform the group that if someone does touch the rope, he or she must start again.

Make these rules: No diving, jumping, or risk taking that may injure yourself or someone else. The team must be in contact with the person going over at all times. No individual effort. Also, no jumping over the rope from a height. Adjustable rules: You may allow people to start on both sides of the rope as long as everyone goes over. Also: make it clear that anyone can choose not to participate. Ask those who "sit out" to participate by being a spotter and *encourager.* Later, discuss:

•*How is getting handed over a rope like, and unlike, receiving an encouraging compliment?*
•*When did you last receive such encouragement?*
•*In general, would you say that such an experience—of being encouraged by someone—is common, or quite rare?*

2—Looking to the Word
(20-25 minutes)

Present the material found in "Presenting What the Bible Has to Say," on pages 84-86.

3—Applying It to My Life
(10-20 minutes)

Needed: A pencil for each group member.

Once you complete your presentation, get everyone started on the "Encouragement Ratings" activity on Interactive Page #2. Have group members work in triads and tell them them that once they circle a number, they must *share specific examples of times when they were encouraging to another person.* What effect did this have?

4—Taking the Next Step
(10-15 minutes)

Needed: A marker and paper for each person.

Give everyone a sheet of paper and a marker. Ask each group member to write an insult on the paper. Preferably, it should be a real-life example of something they've heard said to them or to another person.

Then form a circle, wad up the papers, and on signal, throw the wadded insults at one another. Each person retrieve one wad, and open it in order to study it for a minute. Then have people read aloud (one at a time) the insult and then state: "How I could respond in a way that might..."

•make friends with the insulter, or
•disarm the situation and make light of it, or
•turn the insult into a compliment.

5—Let's Wrap It Up
(5-10 minutes)

Clean up the "insult wads" by throwing them—from a distance—in the trash. Then pray together that you will all "trash" any desire to put people down in your group. Pray for a spirit of encouragement to permeate all you do together.

HINT:

Plan the timing of each step on your "Game Plan" worksheet. Allow 2-3 minutes per response for discussion interaction. Expect everything to take more time than planned, so don't plan too much. Have a back-up option or two ready in the rare event that discussions move quicker than anticipated.

1—Let's Get Started
(20-30 minutes)

Option 1: Olympic Luge
Needed: Chalkboard, dry-erase board or overhead projector, with a blank sheet and a marker/chalk.

On the chalkboard, draw a single line that will serve as an imaginary luge course. Include left/right turns, uphill (arrow pointing up on the board next to the line), downhill (arrow pointing down on the board) and start/finish lines.

Get everyone into teams of three or four people. The team members will sit on the floor, one right after the other, as if they are sitting on a toboggan. As you use the pointer to trace the "course," team members will lean in the direction of the course, all together, so it looks like they are really going down the course.

Do the course three times, all the teams going together on your command. Encourage teamwork and synchronism. The first time should be a slow practice. After the event, ask:

•*How would a real luge team have to pull together in order to win?*

•*How do we—as a singles group— have to pull together in order to "win"?*

•*What role does encouragement play in pulling together? Share an example.*

Option 2: Body English
Challenge a group of eight to ten people to spell out words or sentences to the rest of the group. You may want to use one "warm up" word and then give the group one of the Key Concepts for the lesson. The group will use their bodies to form words and sentences. make participants be a little more creative by not allowing the use of hands. This is a great way to get focused on what you're going to speak about.

Option 3: Quote Reactions
Distribute the Take Home page and direct attention to "In Other Words." Assign small groups one of the quotes about encouragement. Ask them too offer a personal reaction or application to the quote.

2—Looking to the Word
(20 minutes)

Present the material found in "Presenting What the Bible Has to Say," on pages 84-86. Divide your allotted time into three segments: (1) Introduction, (2) Key Concepts, and (3) Conclusion. Keep your presentation short and to the point, drawing upon the "Going Deeper" information as appropriate.

3—Applying It to My Life
(30-40 minutes)

Needed: Paper, pencils, large poster board or butcher paper.

Split the group up into teams of five. Have the groups come up with a Top Ten list of reasons why we should encourage each other. Have them turn in their lists, and then make up a poster board with all of the reasons listed. Put the poster board up on the wall!

4—Taking the Next Step
(30 minutes)

Direct everyone to the "Encouragement Ideas" section of the Take Home Page. Together, decide on one of the ideas there —or any practical variation— that you will all commit to implementing. Plan who, when, where—in detail—as a way to take the next step.

5—Let's Wrap It Up
(5 minutes)

Needed: Index cards, pencils, small bowl or box.

1. Have each person jot down a need that they have on an index card. Put the cards in a box or bowl, and have each person grab one. Pray for the need listed.

2. Make your group's announcements at this time, then close with a benediction of encouragement.

My Personal Game Plan

STEP 1   Time: _____ minutes.

Materials Needed:

Activities Summary:

STEP 2   Time: _____ minutes.

Materials Needed:

Activities Summary:

STEP 3   Time: _____ minutes.

Materials Needed:

Activities Summary:

STEP 4   Time: _____ minutes.

Materials Needed:

Activities Summary:

STEP 5   Time: _____ minutes.

Materials Needed:

Activities Summary:

Just for You
Teacher's Devotional

Ever feel like giving up? As I (Kent) think through the people who have influenced my life for the Kingdom over the years, my mind fills with sweet memories. I don't remember a lot of the things those people said to me. But I do remember their faces and many of their names. And I especially recall that they dedicated vast swatches of time in their lives to serve God—and to love me.

And somehow they kept on doing it, year after year.

Don't think for a minute that your singles don't notice the fact that you are "taking the time" to serve them. They do, and they will remember your sacrifice. Yet it's easy to lose heart as a teacher or leader of a ministry. We can begin to wonder: *Is all of this sacrifice worth it? Am I making any difference at all?*

The answer is: "Let us not become weary in doing good: for at the proper time we will reap a harvest, if we do not give up" (Gal. 6:9). There are rewards here. And the harvest time is coming! So, take a moment to recall the goodness, the past successes, the rewards to come. Let these things spur you on in your commitment as you prepare for another meeting.

Let me remind myself: In spite of the hard work and the occasional discouragements, what are some of the rewards of my ministry to singles?

- _____
  _____

- _____
  _____

- _____
  _____

- _____
  _____

- _____
  _____

—Joel and Kent

MY GOALS FOR THIS SESSION:

- **TO HELP SINGLE ADULTS**
  _____
  _____
  _____

- **TO HELP SINGLE ADULTS**
  _____
  _____
  _____

- **TO HELP SINGLE ADULTS**
  _____
  _____
  _____

- **TO HELP SINGLE ADULTS**
  _____
  _____
  _____

WHAT I LEARNED FROM READING 'LOOKING TO THE WORD' . . .

Notes and Insights—

83

LOOKING TO THE WORD—A ZEALOUS AND OUTRAGEOUS ENCOURAGEMENT

Presenting What the Bible Has to Say...

H ere's your mini-lecture covering the biblical Key Concepts. Make it your own by adding personal anecdotes, to the points, subpoints, and illustrations provided. Special instructions to you are in bold type.

Introduction

Bring in some face paints. Split your group into several small groups.

Remind everyone that we have all seen the people on TV who go to sports activities and paint their faces. They get wild and crazy about their team. Have each small group pick a person and paint his or her face. After a few minutes, have the "paintees" come up front to show the entire group. Judges may decide who has the best painted face. Give that person a crazy prize.

THE KEY CONCEPTS

Transition statement: We live in a world where encouragement is hard to come by. These crazy people on TV are willing to go to great lengths to root for their team. Some of them even paint letters all over their stomachs parts (Wouldn't that have been fun to do today?). They have absolutely no shame about their cause and who they are rooting for.

In the same way, we as a body, a team, need to be constantly rooting wildly and encouraging each other. In an emotional, and social sense, we need to be painting our faces for one another. Today I would like to talk with you about having a zealous and outrageous encouragement for each other.

Read Hebrews 10:24-25 aloud.

The point is: When we embrace the ministry of encouragement, true community surfaces. Therefore, let us—

•Zealously believe in one another.
•Outrageously build up one another.

KEY CONCEPT #1: BIBLICAL Let us zealously believe in one another.

Illustration. When David Livingstone, the great British missionary to Africa, first attempted to preach, he failed miserably—overcome with stage fright. He walked to the pulpit and said: "Friends, I have forgotten all I had to say." In shame he stepped from the pulpit! At that moment, Robert Moffat, who was visiting Edinburgh, advised David not to give up. Perhaps he could become a doctor instead of a preacher, he advised. Livingstone decided to be both. When the years of medical study were done, he went to Africa and greatly influenced that continent for Christ.

Moffat zealously believed in his young friend. What does that mean, in practical terms today? Let me suggest:

(1) It means encouraging each other to "not give up." As singles, you know that life can get lonely and rough. It is so crucial to have a team of people in our lives that serve as our "Robert Moffats."

(2) It means saying: "I believe in you." Don't stop there, however. Keep on saying things like: "I'm proud of you; you can make it; you are awesome." When I zealously believe in you, I'm not afraid to say those kinds of things. I understand that they are medicine to your soul.

(3) It means support in the tough times. We can zealously believe in each other by standing up and supporting our team mates in times of struggle and pain. I would like to ask you a question today: How many of you in here are struggling with something small or large in your life right now? The hands that go up should show you how important it is to believe in one another.

(4) It means having a "righteous jealousy" for one another. It is being committed to one another—not judging, not guessing about motives, not tearing down one another.

Here's a neat quotation that sums it all up nicely: "'No man is an island,' said poet John Donne. I believe every person is an island, but there are no limits to the bridges or harbors one can build."—Roy C. Cook

• *What kinds of bridges or harbors have people made for you over the years?*

• *Who has clearly believed in you, and what difference has it made?*

• *Think: Who might be waiting for a word of encouragement, or an indication of "believing in," from you today?*

KEY CONCEPT #2:
Let us outrageously build up one another.

Illustration. Grab one of your singles and place him or her in a chair in front of the group. Tell everyone that you are all going to take about three minutes to "outrageously build up" that person. Instruct the group to offer words of affirmation, encouragement, love, compliments, assurances of prayer, etc. The goal is for the person in the chair to feel "built up" after the exercise.

Now read Thessalonians 5:11 aloud and make these two points:

(1) "Building up" ought to be a lifestyle. Let's understand that we are all very fragile people. We all have deep needs for love and encouragement. As a body, a team, we should be building each other up consistently. There shouldn't have to be a specific exercise, like the one we just did, in order for us to build each other up. It should be a lifestyle for us, a value that we display whenever we are together.

(2) "Building up" is a craft that has its own tools.
Building each other up means being consumed with meeting each other's needs. And there are certain tools that we can employ in order to do it well. They are: Time (being willing to spend an evening or day together); Touch (a physical touch is a building block); Trust (when we are vulnerable, and willing to share with each other in confidence); Truth (when we can give each other honest input and loving confrontation).

Conclusion
Remember our beginning sports illustration? Some of us feel as though we are insignificant players in this game called Life. We put on our uniform every day and go out there to sweat it out. We can sometimes wonder if anyone ever notices, or if anyone is out there cheering for us. Believing in each other, and building each other up requires all of us to be cheer leaders. It requires us to "put on the paint" for each other and go hog wild!

When we can become an encouraging body, God will do great and mighty works among us. People in this room will begin to understand that they are not alone, that there is a cheerleading squad yelling for them—every day.

GOING DEEPER

"Encouragement" in New Testament Greek.

Here are some of the Greek words that translate into the English word "encouragement":

Protrepo (verb): to urge forward; used in Acts 18:27.

Paramutheomai (verb): to counsel or advise; translated "encouraging" in 1 Thessalonians 2:11, and "encourage" in 5:14 (there signifying to stimulate to the discharge of ordinary life duties). In John 11:19, 31, it means "to comfort."

Paraklesis (noun): a calling alongside to someone's aid (*para*, "by the side"; *kaleo*, "to call"). It's translated "encouragement" in Hebrews 6:18.

Hebrews 10:24-25. As you meditate on this passage, consider the privileges you gain when you come to Christ: (1) personal access to the father. (2) the ability to grow in faith, overcome doubts and questions, and deepen our relationship with Him; (3) the enjoyment of encouragement from one another (10:24); (4) the goodness of worshiping together. If we neglect to meet together for worship, we are forsaking the opportunity to give and receive encouragement—something crucial to each of us fighting daily Kingdom battles.

OTHER ENCOURAGING PASSAGES—

- Romans 15:5. God gives encouragement.
- 1 Samuel 23:16. Jonathan strengthened David's hand.
- 2 Chronicles 30:22. Hezekiah spoke encouragingly to the Levites.
- Deuteronomy 3:28. Encourage Joshua.
- 2 Samuel 11:25. Encourage Joab.
- 1 Thessalonians 5:11. Encourage one another.
- Hebrews 3:13. Encourage daily.
- Titus 2:15. Encourage and reprove with all authority.
- Philippians 1:14. The brethren encouraged to speak the Word.
- Matthew 9:2. Take courage, my son.
- Acts 27:25. Be of good courage, for I believe God.

EXTRA OPTIONS

Pick and Choose any of the following to fit the needs of your group...

1. Fishing with their hands.
2. Blowing their nose.
3. Doing what they do at work.
4. Studying the Bible.
5. Bowling backwards.
6. Playing their favorite sport.

Options to Consider...for Step 1

Group Juggle—The object is to work together to perfect this group skill: juggling one tennis ball around a circle as quickly as possible. Begin by instructing your group to form a circle. Have each person raise their hand until they have the ball thrown to them. Give the ball to the first person and tell her to keep her hand raised to be the last one to get the ball (Start and Finish). Also, encourage each person to call out the name of the person he is going to throw it to.

The ball travels around to each person in the group. Tell everyone to remember who they threw it to. Now have them do the whole process, working for the best time possible. Ask:

•How is "juggling by group" like, and unlike, "growing by group" (growing spiritually, that is—and growing in community)? What part does mutual encouragement play?

Situational Encouragement—Have some volunteers get up in front of the group to do certain tasks. Tell the rest of the group to be encouraging to these "actors," no matter what. Assign one or two people to act out these situations, with the rest being encouragers:

Options to Consider...for Step 3

Build Me Up—Bring in a deck of cards and have everyone form groups of three. Have the groups build the largest card house possible. The idea is to get as many cards standing as possible. Tell the group, after they have completed their houses, to blow them down.

Then make this point: In our relationships here, we can be tempted to blow down rather than build up. The building of up of each other is a fragile process, much like the building of a card house. We must understand that each of us are fragile people, and need to be built up on a daily basis.

HINT:

Interested in a book with some more great activities? I would suggest two books by Project Adventure, Inc.: *Silver Bullets*, by Karl Rohnke and *Quicksilver*, by Karl Rohnke and Steve Butler. Call to order: (508) 468-7981.

The "Spur Me On" Board—Create a bulletin board on the wall that is used to spur one another on. Instruct your participants to write out some short notes of encouragement. Have them put the names of the people on the front of the notes. To get them started, you can write notes to a few of your singles. Pin them to the board, and in front of everyone go to the board and read some of them aloud.

Whatever Comes to Mind—Split the group into teams of five. Have each person in the small groups respond with whatever comes into their minds when you speak certain phrases. Here are some statements to use:

- I love you.
- I believe in you.
- What is your problem?
- I can't stand him.
- You are an awesome person.
- I need you to care about me.
- You are very gifted.

Come up with some others if the above statements don't fit your needs. But use the activity to make the point that our words to one another matter greatly. They generate immediate responses within us. And the things we say have the power to give LIFE!

Options to Consider…for Step 4

Encouragement Party—Choose two to four people in your group that have been going through some tough times. Tell them that on a certain evening the group will be throwing an Encouragement Party for them. At the party, make sure to have their favorite food and drink. Show their favorite movie that night. Develop an activity specifically designed to build them up!

Parental Freedom Night—Announce in church that the singles group will be offering free baby sitting on a certain Friday night, so the parents can go out on a date. Make sure parents signup, though, or you may get overtaken by takers!

Options to Consider…for Step 5

Encouraging "Words" Prayer—Have your singles join hands in a circle and use these words to encourage each other in their prayers: build, love, support!

Love Songs Closing—Sing love songs to God during a brief time of worship. Let this time be quite spontaneous, a time when people choose to sing their favorite worship songs, with or without accompaniment. It might help to have some song books ready, or sing old camp songs that everyone knows. Point out: One of the greatest encouragements for any Christian is to take the opportunity to worship God together with fellow believers.

BIBLE TEXT

Therefore encourage one another and build each other up, just as in fact you are doing.
—1 Thessalonians 5:11

And let us consider how we may spur one another on toward love and good deeds. 25 Let us not give up meeting together, as some are in the habit of doing, but let us encourage one another—and all the more as you see the Day approaching.
—Hebrews 10:24-25

WHADDAYA THINK?

1. In your opinion, is it more natural for human beings to "tear each other down," or "build each other up"? Explain.

2. Why is encouragement so powerful? When has it been powerful for you, personally?

3. What person or persons have really encouraged and built you up over the years? How did they do it?

4. How can we zealously believe in each other? What does that look like in real life?

5. How can we outrageously build up one another? What does that look like?

KEY CONCEPTS
on Encouragement

#1 Let us zealously _____in one another.

#2 Let us outrageously _____up one another.

WHEN I REALLY NEED IT...

Rank the items below from 1 to 10, in the order of your greatest need for encouragement.

The times when I need encouragement the most are . . .

___ when I'm all alone.
___ when holidays come around, and I'm far from home.
___ when I get put down at work.
___ when I consider my(circle one): spiritual life / social life / emotional life.
___ when I'm struggling with physical limitations.
___ when I compare my level of "success" with others my age.
___ when I arrive home after a date.
___ when I try to handle daily problems and difficulties.
___ when I don't understand what God is trying to do.
___ when nobody seems to understand me—who I really am.

•*One way this group can help fill my need for encouragement is...*

_____

_____

_____

Therefore encourage one another and build each other up, just as in fact you are doing.
—1 Thessalonians 5:11

And let us consider how we may spur one another on toward love and good deeds. 25 Let us not give up meeting together, as some are in the habit of doing, but let us encourage one another—and all the more as you see the Day approaching.
—Hebrews 10:24-25

ENCOURAGING TRUTHS?

Why should we encourage one another around here? Mark the following statements True or False.

___ because we rarely get encouragement anywhere else.

___ because most people in this group know and like each other pretty well.

___ because we'll be obeying God if we do.

___ because we can get what we want if we're nice to others.

___ because conflict is a bad thing.

___ because God is pleased with us and enjoys who we are.

___ because God is basically down on us, and wants us to shape up.

___ because it's generally better to be nice, no matter what.

___ because most people in this group need it.

KEY CONCEPTS
on Encouragement

1. Let us zealously _____in one another.

2. Let us outrageously _____up one another.

ENCOURAGEMENT RATINGS

When it comes to being an encourager, how would you rate yourself?
(Circle a number on the line below, and be ready to explain your response.)

1   2   3   4   5   6   7   8   9   10

"Never a discouraging word" passes by my lips.

"Outta my face, you hockey puck."

TIME FOR A RESPONSE

The most personally relevant thing I've learned in this session is:

[ ]

What can I do to put feet to this principle this week?

In my time with God:

In my personal life:

In my church/personal ministry:

In my community:

In my workplace:

In my friendships:

As a single parent (teaching this principle to my kids):

With my roommate(s):

Encouragement Ideas

This Call's for You—Meet as a group in a church office or business with two or three open phone lines you can use. Talk about the importance of encouraging each other through good communication. Brainstorm a list of church workers, teachers, and volunteers in the community. Have participants take turns phoning them and thanking them for what they do in your city. For fun, have pizza delivered. Overwhelm the delivery person with your thanks and appreciation.

Notable Notes—Put up a list of people in the church who need encouraging. Have some official "Thank You" and "Encouragement" cards printed with the singles group or church logo on them. Make them available at the end of the meeting and let your group members know that if they write the notes, you will deliver them.

Project Pastor—Find out some of the things your pastor needs and brainstorm how you can help. Get a few people together and go encourage your pastor. Tell him or her of your gratitude (be prepared to name specific aspects of his or her ministry that you particularly appreciate.)

Videotaped Encouragement—Think about one or more of your singles who are absent from your meeting. Have the group say words of encouragement to those persons—in videotaped "snippets." Have volunteers deliver the tapes during the week.

IN OTHER WORDS . . .

The greatest hater of a man's soul, Satan, knows that his turf is threatened by the safety and power of brotherhood. The forces of evil will do everything they can to separate a man from others, to force him into a place where he's starved for the encouragement, the correction, the prayer—the love— of the men of God.
—Brian Peterson, in *New Man magazine*

There is no such thing as a "self-made" [person]. We are made up of thousands of others. Everyone who has ever done a kind deed for us, or spoken one word of encouragement to us, has entered into the make-up of our character and of our thoughts, as well as our success.
—George Matthew Adams

(CONTIUES FLIPSIDE)

Take Home Page  continued

continued

People have a way of becoming what you encourage them to be—not what you nag them to be.
—Scudder N. Parker, *The Heart and Soul of Leadership*

DAILY READINGS AND REFLECTIONS
Make journal entries related to the following verses each day. Why not spend some time praying them into your life?

Monday—Romans 12:15. Paul exhorts the believer to rejoice and mourn with all of those who rejoice and mourn, not specifically Christians. Ask God to help you open up your emotions to all those around you, showing you care.

Tuesday—Ephesians 4:29. Paul is quite direct about building up and not tearing down others with our talk. In what ways can this verse control your language all day?

Wednesday—Philemon 1:7. Paul talks about love being such an encouragement to him. How could you love someone in a way that they would feel encouraged today?

Thursday—Galatians 6:2. Paul talks here about carrying each other's burdens. When was the last time that you carried someone's burden? How could you do that with someone today?

Friday—Hebrews 10:24-25. Paul encourages believers to spur each other on to good deeds. What would it mean for you to spur someone on to a good deed today?

Saturday—Philippians 2:4. Paul exhorts the believers not to be selfish. In what ways have you been selfish lately? How could you give your selfishness to God today?

GETTING CLOSER
•**Climbing Wall.** Take the group to an indoor or outdoor climbing wall and have everyone suit up in a harness and give it a try! But the key to the whole experience is not individual success—it is group encouragement. Cheer on everyone as they climb, so it as if they have a fan club.

•**Ropes Course.** Find a nearby Ropes Course in your area for team building fun. Many Christian camps have a ropes course, or they could refer you to one. For more information, call: Christian Camping International, (719) 260-9400.

•**Cheer Up.** Attend a sports event or other activity that one of your fellow singles group members is involved in. Cheer them on! Let them know that they matter to you.

JOURNALING SUGGESTIONS
Now it is time to listen, to slow down long enough to hear God's still, small voice. Scripture says, "Be still, and know that I am God" (Ps. 46:10). It's these quiet moments after prayer and listening that really matter. They nourish authentic Christianity. Power flows out of stillness, strength out of solitude. Decisions that change the course of lives come out of these quiet times.

Begin your journaling time with these words: "Lord, You talked to Your children all through history, and You said You're an unchangeable God. Talk to me now. I'm listening. I'm open."

Ask God the following questions:

•What is my next step in my relationship with You?
•What's the next step in the development of my character?
•What's the next step in my relationships/ dating life?
•What's the next step in my ministry?
•What is my next step in my vocation/career?

Over time you'll become more adept at sensing God's answers to these questions. You'll receive Scripture verses, ideas, or insights that are just what you need. Those moments of inspiration will become precious memories you carry with you all day.

—adapted from *Authenticity* by Bill Hybels (Grand Rapids, MI: Zondervan Publishers)